Women Aviators

Women Aviators

26 Stories of Pioneer Flights, Daring Missions, and Record-Setting Journeys

Karen Bush Gibson

CHICAGO
REVIEW
PRESS

Cover and interior design: Sarah Olson
Front cover photos: (*top*) Nancy Love (National Archives); (*bottom, from left to right*)
Bessie Coleman (San Diego Air and Space Museum); Neta Snook (Ames Historical
Society); Hazel Ying Lee (Courtesy of Texas Women's University Women's
Collection); Willa Brown (National Archives)
Interior photos: Alaska Aviation Museum: p. 161; Ames Historical Society: p. 32;
Biblioteque Nationale de France: p. 84; Bundesarchiv: p. 125 (Bild 183-B02092/
Schwahn/CC-BY-SA); Chicago History Museum, *Chicago Daily News* Negatives
Collection: p. 75; International Women's Air & Space Museum: p. 192; Library of
Congress: p. 6 (LC-USZ62-129830); 8 (LC-USZ62-107402); 16 (LC-USZ62-15070); 22
(LC-USZ62-45024); 46 (LC-USZ62-20901); 172 (LC-DIG-npcc-17217); NASA: p. 67;
National Archives: p. 90 (#535717); National Association of College and University
Halls: p. 148; Newark Public Library: p. 142; Polar First/Jennifer Murray: p. 186;
Public Domain: p. 118; San Diego Air and Space Museum: p. 25; 55; 61; 72; 79; 136;
155; 179; Texas Women's University: p. 81; 197; US Air Force: p. 99; 103; 104; 115;
Veterans History Project: p. 111

The Library of Congress has cataloged the hardcover edition as follows:
Gibson, Karen Bush.
  Women aviators : 26 stories of pioneer flights, daring missions, and record-setting
journeys / Karen Bush Gibson. — 1st ed.
     p. cm.
  Includes bibliographical references and index.
  Audience: 12+
  ISBN 978-1-61374-540-3 (cloth)
  1. Women air pilots—Biography—Juvenile literature. 2. Women air pilots—
History—Juvenile literature. I. Title.

TL539.G53 2013
629.13092'52—dc23

                              2013007554

≣ CONTENTS ≣

≡ INTRODUCTION ≡

AT THE TURN OF THE LAST century, two brothers ran a bicycle shop in Dayton, Ohio. They had a dream of creating a machine heavier than air that could fly in the sky. Although they tried many experiments, they were often greeted by failure. But every time they failed, they would learn something that brought them closer to success. They built a glider in 1902. Then they created a gasoline engine to put in a flyer. Finally, the Wright Brothers developed a successful airplane that first lifted off from Kitty Hawk, North Carolina, on December 17, 1903.

The story of the Wright Brothers' first flight is a familiar story, but mention Katherine Wright and you're likely to get a blank look. Yet without Katherine Wright, it's questionable whether Wilbur and Orville Wright would have succeeded.

As the youngest child and only girl in the Wright family, Katherine was forced to grow up quickly after the death of the mother from tuberculosis. Only fifteen, it became her job to take care of the family. She was particularly close to Wilbur and Orville, who were closer to her age than the two older Wright brothers. She was the only one of the Wright children to finish college.

Katherine arranged for volunteers to help her brothers with the flying machine. She later quit her job to care for Orville, who had been badly hurt in a crash. She managed her brothers' business affairs and became an officer in their company. Katherine had far better social skills than her brothers, which also helped their airplane receive the right kind of attention. The French were so taken with Katherine that they called her the "third Wright brother" and awarded her and her brothers the Legion of Honor.

As soon as people were convinced that airplanes and flight were possible, they were interested in flying and building airplanes. Aviation took off with the most adventurous souls ready to lead the charge.

To the surprise of many men, there were women who wanted to pilot these new flying machines as well. Some men didn't think women had either the physical strength or the mental capacity to pilot an airplane. Women had to prove themselves, again and again by earning pilot licenses, setting records, demonstrating aerial moves, and winning races. They had to keep proving themselves, because as Ambassador Clare Boothe Luce once wrote, "Because I am a woman, I must make unusual efforts to succeed. If I fail, no one will say, 'She doesn't have what it takes.' They will say, 'Women don't have what it takes.'"

Today, women pilots fly for the airlines, in the military, and in space. They fly air races, command helicopter mercy flights, haul freight, stock high mountain lakes with fish, seed clouds, patrol pipelines, teach others to fly, maintain jet engines, and transport people.

Whether male or female, people become pilots often for the same reasons. First, they love flying, and they love using their talents and being respected for them. They enjoy the feeling of belonging to this strong family called aviation. Perhaps most of all, they love the challenge of being in the air, because there's nothing else like it.

PART I

Pioneers of Aviation

Great change came with the beginning of the 20th century. The Machine Age led to the creation of factories. People left the uncertainty of rural agricultural life for the many jobs that factories and machinery provided. The cities pulsated with life from the bright lights, radio, and new motion pictures.

The steam engine made it possible to transport people and goods great distances, whether by train or boat. Transportation possibilities blew wide open when Henry Ford opened Ford Motor Company in 1903. Now people had personal transportation that they could take out whenever they wanted. What could be next?

Even with the vast amount of progress in the world, a heavier-than-air flying machine was still a surprise. Flying was something that had to be seen to be believed, so people flocked to airfields and exhibitions to be amazed.

After aviation was introduced, its popularity spread quickly, and soon countries such as France, Great Britain, and Germany began investing in this new and wondrous industry. France in particular began producing great pilots, airplanes, and flight schools, so it's not surprising that the first licensed woman pilot was French. In fact, five of the first six licensed women pilots were French (number four, Hélène Dutrieu, was from Belgium). The first 10 women to earn a pilot's license were the following:

1. Raymonde de Laroche, France—March 8, 1910
2. Marthe Niel, France—August 29, 1910
3. Marie Marvingt, France—November 8, 1910
4. Hélène Dutrieu, Belgium—November 25, 1910
5. Jeanne Herveau, France—December 7, 1910
6. Marie-Louise Driancourt, France—June 15, 1911
7. Harriet Quimby, USA—August 1, 1911
8. Lidia Zvereva, Russia—August 10, 1911
9. Matilde Moisant, USA—August 17, 1911
10. Hilda Hewlett, England—August 29, 1911

Hélène Dutrieu. *Library of Congress: LC-USZ62-129830*

Women's roles in society were changing. No longer content to sit on the sidelines, women wanted to fly. But most men were uneasy about women in planes. Pilots knew that flying a plane had nothing to do with physical strength, but they doubted that women could understand the technology behind aviation. And if there were an emergency, what women could make the calm, rational decisions needed?

But women had exactly what was needed for aviation, and they were determined to join men in the skies. In the early years, getting a pilot's license wasn't a requirement. Women such as Blanche Scott and Bessica Raiche were reportedly flying before America's first woman pilot earned a license, but neither woman stayed with aviation. Raiche became a physician. Scott became disgusted with the industry after seeing the public's attraction to plane crashes.

The people who pursued aviation, both men and women, were truly remarkable. Most airplanes weren't very sturdy and didn't offer much protection in a crash. American women, who weren't even allowed to vote until 1920, had to work hard just to find someone to teach them how to fly, as most flight schools didn't accept female students.

Seven years after Wilbur Wright flew 120 feet (36.5 meters) in the flyer, women were demanding the opportunity to fly. The early female aviation pioneers made things possible for the women who followed. They were the first.

≣ BARONESS DE LAROCHE ≣

"Bird Woman"

PEOPLE AT THE AÉRO-CLUB in the Reims-Bétheny region of France were enjoying a lovely day with comfortable temperatures and a light breeze. For centuries, Reims, located northeast of Paris, was the city where French kings had been crowned. It was a city of important people. Most Saturdays brought the wealthy of Reims to the Aéro-Club to see the new airplanes being flown. People were fascinated that a flimsy machine made of wood and canvas could leave the ground—and with a person inside, too.

Suddenly, a woman moved through the crowd in a way that said she was someone important. Whispers of "baroness" floated through the air as she stopped a few times to speak with different people.

All eyes remained on this baroness as she moved toward one of the airplanes. Almost everyone looked confused as she laced a string around the hem of her dress. At the front of the dress, she tried the string as if she were tying a shoe. Someone said aloud, "That's to keep her dress from flying up."

Even more surprising was what she did next. She quickly hopped into the seat of the plane. After the gasps subsided, a silence settled over the crowd. Then a mechanic stepped to the front of the plane. Reaching as high as he could, he pulled the propeller down. He repeated this motion a few more times until the engine sputtered to life and the propeller spun on its own.

More than a few faces looked around, expecting someone to stop the woman. No one did. The plane moved forward along the ground, gradually moving faster until it lifted off. The stunning vision prompted wild applause from the audience. The woman made a few turns above the airfield before landing smoothly on the ground.

By that time, everyone knew the name of Baroness de Laroche, the first woman in the world to earn a pilot's license.

———•———

Elise Raymonde Deroche was born in Paris, France, on August 22, 1886. The daughter of a plumber, she was not born a baroness. She was, however, born with a sense of adventure. Her sense of style and commanding appearance led to some success on the stage as an actress. She even changed her name to the more dramatic Raymonde de Laroche.

But life as an actress didn't meet Elise's thirst for adventure. The two-wheeled contraption known as the velocipede became popular in France in the late 1860s. It would later become known as the bicycle. Elise taught herself to ride one before moving on to balloons.

Hot-Air Balloons

People first "flew" in the sky by hot-air balloons a little over a hundred years before Elise was born. Another French citizen, Jean-François Pilâtre de Rozier, invented the first manned balloon in 1783. Although de Rozier and his friend, the Marquis d'Arlandes, were the first humans in a balloon, a duck actually made the first historic flight when de Rozier put one in the basket for a 15-minute flight.

The balloon was heated with a straw fire, which caused the air in the balloon to expand—and frequently to catch on fire. Like airplanes, however, balloons improved, progressing to a helium and hot-air system. The first balloon flight across the English Channel was in 1785. Balloons appeared in America by 1793. President George Washington witnessed a balloon's first US flight. Balloons later proved useful during the Civil War and World Wars I and II. In earlier wars, they were used for observation. Leaders could see for miles around, which helped them to develop their strategies. By the time airplanes were used in war, militaries would tether barrage balloons to the ground to limit the visibility of low-flying enemy planes.

Elise loved the feeling of soaring high in the air and looking down upon the earth. She soon became an accomplished balloonist in a time when women balloonists were rare.

Her interest in flying grew when she heard that an American named Wilbur Wright would be arriving in France to demonstrate his new flyer. On August 8, 1908, Wright arrived in Le Mans, a city between Paris and the west coast of France. Only five years earlier, Wilbur and his brother Orville had tested the first flyer in Kitty Hawk, North Carolina.

A team of horses hauled the Wright flyer onto the center of a racetrack near Le Mans. The audience watched as a couple of men pulled down on the propeller. Suddenly the propeller began moving very fast by itself. At the same time, the flyer began moving forward. Wilbur Wright took off and flew around the racetrack. Not only did he dazzle the crowd in the stands, but he also amazed the French officials who had said that a flying machine was an impossibility. After he landed, Wilbur offered rides to any women in the audience interested in experiencing flight. There was no way Elise would miss this opportunity.

After she had flown with Wilbur Wright, ballooning no longer appealed to Elise. Luckily, the French took to aviation quickly. Within a year, Elise was asking Charles Voisin, a French aviator, to teach her to fly. Voisin and his brother, Gabriel, built and flew airplanes. Voisin agreed to teach the 23-year-old actress how to fly.

Their airplane, called the Voisin, was a single-seater aircraft, which meant the teacher had to teach from outside the airplane. For her first lesson, Charles Voisin showed Elise how to move, or taxi, the airplane down the field. The noise of the airplane was loud. He shouted for her to try it but warned her to stay on the ground.

Elise took her first lesson in Châlons, about 147 miles (237 kilometers) east of Paris. First, she taxied the small airplane down the airfield. When she reached the end, a waiting mechanic turned the plane around, and she taxied back. Then Charles turned her around and told her to do it again. This time, Elise opened up the throttle, rising about 15 feet (4.5 meters) in the air. She flew a few hundred yards, made a gentle landing, and came taxiing back to her starting point.

Charles Voisin must have realized that Elise had a talent for piloting, because he kept teaching her, even though she had defied him. She continued to improve, and the two became very close.

Early airplanes weren't very sturdy, and accidents were common. Elise didn't allow her first accident in early 1910 to stop her. As she approached her landing at Châlons, a strong gust of wind hit her plane, causing her to slam into some trees, fall about 20 feet (6 meters), and break her collarbone. After her injury healed, she left with the Voisin brothers for Egypt to compete in the Heliopolis air meet. Bad weather kept some aviators from competing, but not Elise. She flew through heavy winds and rains to finish in eighth place.

On March 8, 1910, Elise felt she was ready to test for her pilot's license. She flew for the officials at the Fédération Aéronautique Internationale (FAI), and her performance left no question about whether she was equipped to fly an airplane. Elise was granted pilot's license number 36, becoming the first licensed woman pilot in the world. Earning this achievement meant she was allowed to enter any aviation contest. The newspapers called her *"la femme oiseau"* (the bird woman).

Elise left acting behind as she traveled, earning money with flying exhibitions and races. She arrived in the Russian city of Saint Petersburg, where the chimneys spit out so much smoke that air currents became unstable and pilots had a hard time seeing. But Elise went up anyway and circled the small airfield. She later told *Collier's* magazine, "I mounted to a height of 150 meters, being enveloped by the smoke from the factory chimney which surrounded the ground. I flew over houses, then above forests, and turned three times."

Turning off her engine, she glided to a perfect landing in front of Tsar Nicholas II. He was so impressed that he bestowed the title of baroness upon the lovely pilot. Elise, who enjoyed being the center of attention, began to use the title.

Baroness de Laroche encountered smoking chimneys again in Budapest, where she was to race a 68-mile (109 kilometers) course against other pilots. The other pilots—men—refused to fly under such circumstances. The baroness completed the course and came away with first place.

On July 8, just four months after earning her pilot's license, Elise returned to Reims to compete against a field of all men. She was doing well in the competition until the sixth day, when she crashed and broke her arm and both legs. When she regained consciousness in the hospital, she said that another plane had come too close and forced her crash. The pilot of the other plane wasn't disciplined. In fact, some people pointed to the incident as proof that women shouldn't be pilots, stating that women just weren't as capable of flying as men.

Elise's injuries took two years to heal. Many thought her flying days were over, but she began training for the Coup Femina, a competition for women who flew the longest distance solo. But Elise had to pull out of the race when an auto accident left her with severe wounds. Her companion, Charles Voisin, was also in the vehicle, and he died as a result of the incident.

Elise was devastated by the loss of her teacher and romantic interest. As she recovered from the accident, she became more determined than ever to get back into the air. In 1913, she experimented with other airplanes. The Sommer was similar to the Voisin she had been flying, but she liked the Farman. All were biplanes, but the Farman had more power.

On November 25, when she participated in the second Femina competition, she flew 200 miles (322 kilometers) in four hours. She stopped to land only when the plane developed a problem in its gas line. Still, her efforts were enough to win the contest.

Fédération Aéronautique Internationale

When aviation took off in popularity, people realized that an organization was needed to monitor the industry's activity. Three European men joined together to recommend a new institution, the Fédération Aéronautique Internationale, which would regulate the sport of flying. An international aviation conference met in Paris in October 1905 to hammer out the rules.

Founded on October 14, 1905, the FAI awarded pilot's licenses and tracked the world's aviation records. Since the formation of the organization, it has expanded to include all aeronautical activities, and it continues to track aviation records.

The outbreak of World War I in 1914 put Elise's flying career on hold. All airplanes and military pilots were needed for the war. Civilian flying was strictly prohibited. Although Baroness de Laroche volunteered her piloting skills, she was turned down. Instead, she became a chauffeur for the French military, moving items and people from place to place.

As soon as the war ended, the baroness jumped back into flying. She set a woman's altitude record of 13,000 feet (4,000 meters) on June 7, 1919. Three days later, American pilot Ruth Law reached 14,700 feet (4,484 meters). But Baroness de Laroche hadn't gotten to where she was by giving up. Five days later, she reclaimed her record by flying to 15,689 feet (4,785 meters).

More airplanes were filling the skies, and new planes were being unveiled every day. People needed to test these airplanes.

As an experienced 33-year-old pilot, Elise believed she would be an ideal candidate for the first female test pilot. On July 18, she had the chance to ride as a passenger in an experimental Caudron, which was located at the airfield in the coastal town of Le Crotoy. She hoped to learn more about being a test pilot.

However, tragedy struck. The airplane went into a spin that sent it plummeting to the ground. The pilot died on his way to the hospital. Elise Deroche, the world's first licensed woman pilot, died instantly.

LEARN MORE

"Baroness de Laroche" on Early Aviators website, http://earlyaviators.com/edelaroc.htm

"Raymonde De La Roche" on Women in Aviation and Space History website, Smithsonian Air and Space Museum, http://airandspace.si.edu/explore-and-learn/topics/women/roche.cfm

Women Aviators by Bernard Marck (Flammarion, 2009)

⧮ HARRIET QUIMBY ⧯

First Woman to Fly
Across the English Channel

HARRIET QUIMBY WAVED GOOD-BYE to friends and officials at the Dover Airfield in England at 5:30 AM on April 16, 1912. Dressed in her usual hooded, plum-colored, satin flying suit, she climbed into a Blériot monoplane, an airplane with one set of wings. Harriet had never piloted the 50-horsepower, single-seat aircraft; she had borrowed it from Louis Blériot, who was famous for being the first aviator to cross the English Channel.

After days of waiting for the bad weather to clear, Harriet was excited to finally be in the air again. A bit of anxiety stayed with her as she navigated through the foggy skies at an altitude between 1,000 and 2,000 feet (300 to 600 meters). This flight had already sent many pilots to their deaths. Harriet tried to think of the flight as a cross-country flight, not "flying in the fog with an untried compass, in a new untried machine knowing that the treacherous North Sea stood ready to receive me if I drifted only five miles too far out of my course."

Harriet's goal was the small coastal town of Calais, France. Although Calais was only 22 miles (29 kilometers) away, she could not see it through the mist, and she landed 25 miles (40 kilometers) south instead, on the beach at Hardelot, France. She was greeted by smiling fishermen who came running when they saw an airplane land. Friends soon arrived, and they carried Harriet on their shoulders after toasting her with champagne.

The trip had taken 59 minutes. Before many people had opened their eyes that day, America's first female pilot, Harriet

English Channel

The English Channel is a famous stretch of water separating Great Britain from mainland Europe. The 350-mile-long (560 kilometers) waterway connects the North Atlantic Ocean to the North Sea. The Channel, as it is commonly known by the British, was historically used as a trade route. Later, Great Britain's strong defense was in part due to the Royal Navy patrolling its coastline during times of war.

The Channel is now used primarily to travel from England to Europe, either across the water or through the Channel Tunnel below it. The Channel has long been a source of contests, which can involve people swimming across or flying over it by balloon or airplane. Most crossings take place at the narrowest point between Dover, England, and Calais, France.

Quimby, had become the world's first woman to fly across the English Channel.

———•———

When Harriet began making a name for herself, first as a journalist and then as a pilot, she was reported to be the daughter of rich landowners who had sent her to private schools in the United States and Europe. Perhaps Harriet or her mother had wanted to create a new image for Harriet, because the truth was that she came from a struggling farm family and had been educated in public schools.

Born in Michigan in May 1875 to William and Ursula Quimby, Harriet spent her early childhood near Coldwater, Michigan. Although several children were born to the Quimbys, only Harriet and her older sister, Kittie, survived childhood.

William fought for the Union in the Civil War until he became ill. His wife, Ursula, healed him with herbal remedies she was known for creating. When the farm failed in the late 1880s, the family moved to California along with Kittie and her new husband. Harriet and her parents eventually settled in the Oakland–San Francisco area. William worked at different jobs, but the Quimbys continued to struggle financially until William began selling Ursula's herbal remedies.

With her dark hair and engaging personality, Harriet considered being an actress. She spent a little time on the stage in San Francisco before turning to writing. She wrote feature articles for publications such as the *San Francisco Bulletin*. After some success, she moved across the country to New York City.

Succeeding as a journalist, particularly as a female journalist in New York City in 1903, was almost impossible. But Harriet brought strong writing skills, intelligence, and determination with her. After showing her published work, which included theatrical reviews and articles about life in Chinatown, she convinced the editors of *Leslie's Illustrated Weekly* to try her as a contributing writer.

Harriet's first article for the popular newspaper was titled "Curious Chinese Customs." She wrote drama critiques, household tips, and political articles. She profiled everyone from actresses to acrobats. As a friend of noted filmmaker D. W. Griffith, she wrote screenplays as well, seven of which were turned into movies.

Traveling as a photojournalist to Egypt, Mexico, Cuba, Europe, and Iceland broadened Harriet's world even more. *Leslie's Illustrated Weekly* hired Harriet as a staff writer, and she wrote more than 250 articles for the paper during her career. Her talent and success led to assignments full of the excitement she craved. On a visit to the Vanderbilt racetrack, Harriet was taken for a ride at 100 miles per hour in a 120-horsepower Vanderbilt Cup Racer. She bought her own car, which she learned to drive and repair herself.

Speed gave Harriet a thrill, and a few years later she attended the International Aviation Tournament in Belmont Park, New York, to see what airplanes had to offer. She watched one pilot, John Moisant, wreck his plane before getting off the ground. Moisant immediately bought a monoplane from another pilot and won the race. Harriet introduced herself to John, who, with his brother Alfred, ran an aviation school in Long Island, New York. She also met Matilde Moisant, their sister. Harriet and Matilde hit it off and became close friends.

Two months later, John Moisant died at an aviation exhibition in New Orleans when his plane went into a dive. Accidents were common in early aviation, with more than a hundred deaths from aviation by the spring of 1911. But Harriet didn't let that stop her. In May 1911, Harriet and Matilde began classes at the Moisant Aviation School. Most flight schools, including the Wright Brothers Flying School, refused to accept women as students. As soon as the papers learned that two women were learning to fly, it became big news. Harriet focused her writing on aviation and convinced *Leslie's* to let her do a series. Audiences loved her feature articles about learning to fly. In "How a Woman Learns to Fly," Harriet wrote, "It feels like riding in a high powered automobile, minus bumping over the rough roads, continually signaling to clear the way and keeping a watchful eye on the speedometer to see that you do not exceed the limit and provoke the wrath of the bicycle policeman."

On August 1, 1911, Harriet became the first woman in the United States to earn a pilot's license. When her FAI license arrived, she saw that she was Pilot Number 37. A few weeks later, Matilde became the second US woman to earn a license. They were among about ten women in the world who were licensed to fly an airplane.

After getting her license, Harriet designed her own flight suit, what she called a knickerbocker uniform. A month later, she became the first woman to fly at night when she flew over Staten Island, New York. Air exhibitions were very popular, and everyone wanted to see the woman pilot they had read about in *Leslie's*. Harriet flew at meets throughout the United States and Mexico. While she was in Mexico, an idea began to form in her mind.

Since Louis Blériot had first crossed the English Channel in 1909, a few other pilots had followed, including John Moisant. Even more had failed at it. One woman had flown over the English Channel as a passenger, but no woman had flown solo over the channel. Harriet decided she wanted to be first.

She traveled to England on an ocean liner. Unlike Blériot, who flew from France to England, she would fly from England

What Happened to Matilde Moisant?

The second American woman to earn her pilot's license, Matilde Moisant, received hers sixteen days after her friend Harriet Quimby. Together the two women participated in exhibition flights as part of a group of performing pilots called the Moisant International Aviators.

Matilde's first exhibition came about a month after receiving her license. She won a trophy for flying at an altitude of 1,200 feet (366 meters) at the Nassau Boulevard Aviation Meet, beating Harriet. High-altitude flying seemed to be Matilde's specialty, as she demonstrated at meets for the next seven months.

Her family, still grieving over the death of her brother John in an aviation accident, begged her to quit flying. Matilde finally gave in, saying she would quit after one more exhibition flight in Wichita Falls, Texas, on April 14, 1912. As she started to land, her airplane burst into flames because of a fuel-tank leak. The plane crashed. Matilde was pulled out with her clothing on fire, but her heavy wool flying suit saved her from serious burns.

That flight was Matilde's last. Two and a half months later, her good friend Harriet Quimby died when her plane crashed.

to France. She kept quiet about her plans because she didn't want another woman to beat her. The people who knew about her quest tried to talk her out of it; this group included Gustav Hamel, an aviator who offered to pretend to be her by wearing the purple flight suit. She refused but agreed to use a compass for the trip.

Harriet's nighttime flight had been big news, but that wouldn't be the case for the bigger challenge of crossing the English Channel. The *Titanic*, a passenger ship that had left England via the English Channel, hit an iceberg in the Atlantic Ocean and sank. Thus, few noticed the stories about the first woman's solo flight over the 22-mile stretch of water separating Great Britain from the European mainland. The news of the *Titantic* disaster overshadowed everything else.

Three months later, Harriet arrived at the third annual Boston Aero Meet, an event that promised the highest fee yet. When she met with the organizer, William Willard, and his son, the two men tossed a coin to see who would have the honor of a flight with Harriet. The elder Willard won the toss. Harriet took off in her new 70-horsepower, two-seater Blériot plane

Boston Aero Meet, 1910. *Library of Congress*

An Inspiration

Harriet Quimby was a woman who inspired others. One of those she inspired was Amelia Earhart, who had this to say about Harriet: "To cross the Channel in 1912 required more bravery and skill than to cross the Atlantic today. . . . We must remember that, in thinking of America's first great woman flier's accomplishment."

and took her passenger around the lighthouse. Five thousand people watched the plane approach over Dorchester Bay before it suddenly went into a nosedive. Willard fell out of the plane to his death. Harriet looked like she might regain control of the airplane, but she too fell into the shallow waters of Dorchester Bay and died instantly.

What exactly happened continues to be a mystery to this day, although there are theories. Willard, a heavy man, might have stood up or leaned forward, throwing the balance of the airplane off. (There were no seatbelts in Harriet's plane.) A meet official mentioned another possibility: that the plane's cables were caught in the steering.

Harriet Quimby was only 37 years old when she died, but she had achieved so much in her life. In a time when women had few rights—they weren't even allowed to vote—Harriet had two successful careers and supported herself. The first American woman pilot and the first woman to cross the English Channel was truly an aviation pioneer, so in 1991, eighty years after receiving her license, the US government honored her with a stamp in the Pioneers of Aviation series. The 50-cent US airmail stamp depicts a beautiful woman, adorned in purple, smiling as a Blériot monoplane flies in the background.

LEARN MORE

"Harriet Quimby" in *Chasing the Sun*, PBS, www.pbs.org /kcet/chasingthesun/innovators/hquimby.html

Harriet Quimby: America's First Lady of the Air (Aviation History Series) by Anita P. Davis and Ed Y. Hall (Honoribus Press, 1993)

"Harriet Quimby" on Women in Aviation and Space History website, Smithsonian Air and Space Museum, http:// airandspace.si.edu/explore-and-learn/topics/women /Quimby.cfm

⫸ BESSIE COLEMAN ⫷

Queen Bess

BESSIE COLEMAN KNEW WHAT she wanted: she wanted to learn how to fly an airplane. How hard could it be? She was a successful 27-year-old woman in Chicago who had pulled herself, mother, and three younger sisters out of poverty. Knocking on the doors of flight schools, the attractive woman with copper skin asked what it would cost to take flying lessons. Everyone turned her down as a student. Some refused her because she was a woman, others because she was African American. Most flight schools refused her for both reasons. So Bessie saved up money by opening up a chili parlor and, in her spare time, learned to speak French. Her friend, *Chicago Defender* editor Robert Abbott, had told her that the French were more accepting of race and gender.

In November 1920, Bessie sailed to France for a 10-month course at the famed Caudron Brothers' School of Aviation at Le Crotoy, France. Bessie walked the nine miles to the airfield every day for flight lessons in order to save her limited funds. She finished the course in seven months, learning to fly a 27-foot (8.2 meters) biplane with a 40-foot (12 meters) wingspan. It was the French Nieuport Type 82.

On June 15, 1921, Bessie took her test. She flew a five-kilometer course at an altitude of 50 meters (160 feet). She was also required to complete a figure eight and land within 50 meters of a designated spot. She received her license from the Fédération Aéronautique Internationale, becoming the first African American with a pilot's license. She was also the only woman among the 62 candidates who earned licenses during the six-month period.

Chicago Defender

Established in 1905 by Robert Abbott, the goal of this Chicago-based African American newspaper was to recognize African Americans and encourage racial pride. Within five years, the small local paper began attracting national attention, and soon it became the country's leading African American newspaper, boasting the motto "The World's Greatest Weekly." The Chicago Defender profiled famous African Americans and covered controversial topics, such as segregation and lynching.

In 1956, the Chicago Defender became a daily publication and began acquiring other US newspapers. It continues today, reporting the news and championing equality for all.

When Bessie arrived in New York the following September, she was surprised at the attention she received from the newspapers. The Harlem Renaissance had exploded in New York, with attention focused on African American writers and entertainers. Everyone wanted to meet Bessie, who was part of just a handful of American women pilots and the only African American among them. She had always wanted to amount to something, and now she had.

———•———

Bessie Coleman was born January 26, 1892, in the northeast Texas town of Atlanta, the tenth of thirteen children born to Susan and George Coleman. The family moved to Waxahachie, Texas, when she was two years old. George, a tenant farmer, built a three-room house for his family. All the Colemans worked in the cotton fields when it was time for the harvest. The children's schools, which were for African Americans only, even shut down so that every student could work in the fields. The work was backbreaking and earned them little money, and Bessie dreamed of a different life.

When she was seven years old, Bessie's father left for Indian Territory (which later became Oklahoma) to the north of Texas. In addition to being African American, he was at least half Choctaw or Cherokee. George was tired of living life in segregated Texas. In Indian Territory, he would have full citizenship. But Susan refused to uproot the family and follow him.

With her older sons leaving as well, it was up to Susan Coleman to support her four remaining daughters, all of whom were younger than nine years of age. She found a job as a cook and housekeeper with the Jones family, kind employers who sent her home with sacks of flour and meat. The Jones family also had daughters and gave the Coleman girls their hand-me-down clothing. Although many housekeepers lived with the families they worked for in those days, the Jones family allowed Susan to live at home with her children.

Still, Susan worked long hours, so Bessie took care of her sisters and the home. She and her sisters attended a one-room schoolhouse for eight years, walking four miles each way. Bessie's best subject was math. When her sisters fell ill, she had to miss school to care for them. She supplemented her education by borrowing books from the traveling wagon library. Sometimes she acted out the stories for her sisters. Bessie read books such as *Uncle Tom's Cabin* and biographies of famous African Americans such as Booker T. Washington.

When she became a little older, Bessie began making extra money by doing laundry, as her mother did. She picked up the laundry weekly, which often required toting the clothes more than five miles. Susan let Bessie keep the money she earned, and these funds allowed her to go to college—the Colored Agricultural and Normal University (now Langston University) in the all-black town of Langston, Oklahoma. College was expensive, however, and Bessie was forced to drop out after the first semester, when her money ran out.

Bessie briefly returned to Texas but knew the town of Waxahachie had nothing to offer her. As soon as she raised the money, she moved to Chicago, where two of her brothers lived. Walter worked as a Pullman porter. John was reported to be unemployed, but he may have also worked for gangster Al Capone.

Bessie had had enough of housekeeping and laundry jobs. Instead, she found work as a manicurist at a barbershop on State Street. The lively South Side area where she worked, referred to as "the Stroll," was later called Chicago's "Black Wall Street."

Businessmen, gangsters, and jazz musicians were frequent clients of hers.

Both of Bessie's brothers fought in World War I. When they returned, they talked about what they had seen, particularly the airplanes. Her brother, John, teased her about how French women could be pilots, but she couldn't. She didn't think that was right. She decided she would be a pilot.

After Bessie had achieved her goal, she realized that the attention and acclaim were nice, but they didn't pay the bills. They also wouldn't help her achieve her dream of opening an aviation school for African Americans. She knew the only way to make a living from flying would be through entertaining people. Unfortunately, she needed more skills. She returned to Europe for six more months of advanced training in France, Holland, and Germany.

Bessie decided to create an image of herself that would attract attention and help her to make money from flying. With her small height of only five feet, three and a half inches, a dashing military-type uniform made her look important as she made her flying debut on September 3, 1922, at an air show at New York's Curtiss Field. Robert Abbott and his newspaper, the *Chicago Defender*, sponsored the show, calling Bessie, "the world's greatest woman flyer." She did more than just fly overhead—she did figure eights, loop-the-loops, barrel rolls, and other barnstorming tricks guaranteed to draw gasps from the crowds. She became "Queen Bess, Daredevil Aviatrix."

Word of "Brave Bessie" and "Queen Bess" spread. Whenever she performed, the crowds lined up. Like many barnstormers, she flew an old Jenny (World War I surplus US Army Curtiss JN-4). She concentrated on air shows in the North at first, gradually moving into the segregated South for performances. In 1925, she debuted in her home state of Texas. She performed in

Houston, San Antonio, Dallas, and any small town with a field, even Waxahachie. She drew both white and black crowds, but she put her foot down about the people using segregated gates to enter the show.

Wherever she went, she encouraged women and African Americans to learn to fly. But Bessie still didn't have enough money to open a flight school. Once she had to replace her own airplane after her Jenny crashed when the motor stalled at 300 feet (90 meters). The accident also resulted in a badly broken leg, three broken ribs, and various cuts. As soon as Bessie was able, she began supplementing her income with lectures, parachute jumping, and wing walking. She even opened a beauty shop in Orlando, Florida, to make money.

When the new Jenny she ordered from Curtiss Airfield in Dallas was finally paid off, she had it flown to Jacksonville, Florida, where her next show was to be held on May 1, 1926. The night before the show, she and her mechanic, William Will, took the plane up. Bessie rode as a passenger so that she could look over the side of the plane for good places to make parachute jumps. They were flying at about 80 miles an hour (130 kilometers per hour) at 3,500 feet (1,100 meters). Witnesses noticed an acceleration before the plane went into a nosedive. When the plane flipped, Bessie fell out and died when she hit the ground. Will struggled to gain control of the plane but couldn't. He crashed the plane about a thousand yards from where Bessie's body lay. He later died. Upon investigation, the cause of the crash was found to be a loose wrench that had jammed into the instruments.

In Orlando, more than 5,000 people paid their respects to Bessie before her body traveled by train to Chicago. There, 10,000 more said good-bye to Queen Bess. Only 34 years old, she didn't live to see her dream come true, but it did happen three years later, when the Bessie Coleman Aero Club was established. The school educated many outstanding African American pilots, including Willa Brown and the Tuskegee Airmen.

Bessie Coleman was not forgotten. In 1931 and for many years afterward, the Challenger Air Pilots Association of Chicago and later the Tuskegee Airmen did a flyover of Lincoln Cemetery on Bessie's birthday. Like Harriet Quimby, Bessie was honored with her own postage stamp in 1995. Chicago mayor Richard M. Daley named a major road at O'Hare Airport after her, calling it Bessie Coleman Drive. Today, Bessie Coleman's brief life continues to inspire others.

LEARN MORE

Bessie Coleman website, www.bessiecoleman.com

"Bessie Coleman" on US Centennial of Flight Commission website, www.centennialofflight.gov/essay/Explorers _Record_Setters_and_Daredevils/Coleman/EX11 .htmBessie

"Bessie Coleman" on Ninety-Nines, Inc. International Organization of Women Pilots website, www.ninety -nines.org/index.cfm/bessie_coleman.htm

Queen Bess: Daredevil Aviator by Doris L. Rich and Mae Jemison (Smithsonian Institution Press, 1995)

Up in the Air: The Story of Bessie Coleman (Trailblazer Biographies) by Philip S. Hart (Carolrhoda Books, 1996)

≣ NETA SNOOK ≣

The Woman Who Taught Amelia to Fly

NOT ALL OF AVIATION'S PIONEERS died tragic deaths or set records. Some were just aviators who demonstrated their skills and talent day after day through the work they did with little fanfare. These people were the foundation of early aviation. Anita "Neta" Snook was one of those people. She accomplished much as an early aviator, but this achievement is often overshadowed by the fact that she taught the most famous woman pilot in the world how to fly.

———•———

Neta Snook was born February 14, 1896, in Mount Carroll, Illinois. She had a happy childhood and loving parents. Even as a toddler, she was drawn to anything mechanical. She enjoyed building toy cars and toy boats instead of playing with the usual dolls that girls were expected to enjoy.

The appearance of automobiles during Neta's childhood thrilled both her and her father. He bought a car when she was nine, and they spent many hours driving. Sometimes, her father let her steer from her perch on his lap. They also studied the engine together, learning how it worked and how to make repairs.

One day, Neta and her family went to the county fair. Neta's eyes grew large as she took in a sight she had never seen before: giant balloons in the air. Neta spent her time at the fair watching balloons and the balloonists who flew them. What would it be like to fly? she wondered.

When she was in her teens, Neta's family moved to Ames, Iowa. After completing high school, she continued her education at Iowa State College (later renamed Iowa State University). The agricultural college had added home economics for the new female students being admitted. Neta was required to complete 17 hours of home economics courses before she could study what she really wanted to learn about: combustion engines, mechanical drawing, and machine repair. Until then, she spent much time in the university library reading up on subjects that fascinated her.

While at college, Neta heard about the Curtiss Flying School in Newport News, Virginia. The school had been started by Glenn Curtiss, an aviator and aircraft manufacturer. Neta applied during her second year of college, but the school turned her down. The response was, "No females allowed."

The next year, a newspaper ad caught her attention. The Davenport Aviation School promised to teach anyone to fly for $400. This time, her application was accepted. She may have been the first woman to attend the school, but she was soon accepted as one of the guys, particularly after she pointed out errors in the blueprints of the plane they were building. Her classmates called their redheaded peer "Curly."

The school introduced the students to aviation, but it was a low-budget operation in an abandoned warehouse on the river. The students had to build and maintain the airplanes if they wanted to fly. This requirement suited Neta's mechanical interests just fine, and she took her first flight on July 21, 1917. She climbed to 6,000 feet (1,800 meters). Years later, Neta would still remember racing down the field at the start of that first flight and the moment the tail lifted off the ground.

Initially, Neta's mother was embarrassed about Neta's being in flight school. It just wasn't something women did. Her mother didn't tell the rest of the family, but soon the secret was out. Neta's grandfather, a Civil War veteran, was so excited that his granddaughter was learning to fly that he visited her at school and took his first and only ride in an airplane at the age of 74. After getting her license, Neta would later take her now-proud mother for a ride around Ames.

Unfortunately, a few months after opening, the school shut down after one of the planes crashed, killing the president of the school and injuring the instructor. With only 100 minutes of flying time under her belt, Neta didn't have enough flight time to test for her license. Several of her classmates who were headed to Curtiss Flying School promised to put in a good word for her.

The 21-year-old Neta spent a few weeks at home, unsure of what to do next. At the end of September, she received a letter. With shaking hands, she opened the envelope and read it. She had to read it again to make sure she was reading correctly. The Curtiss Flying School had accepted her. Within the week, she rejoined her classmates.

The school was a good one, and Neta learned a lot. She logged flight time while eagerly awaiting her first solo flight. But before she could take that flight, the US government stopped all flying at the Virginia school. World War I had started, and security officials worried that German spies might enroll in the school as a way to spy on nearby military bases and government.

The airplanes were dismantled, and they and the students were shipped to Miami to continue training. This didn't last long either. About two months later, president Woodrow Wilson issued an order that there would be no private flying in the United States during the war. Neta still hadn't taken her solo flight. With a letter of recommendation from the school, she returned home, a frustrated "almost pilot."

Her frustration didn't last long. One of Neta's classmates recommended her for a job with the British Air Ministry. As an expediter, her job was to oversee the delivery of airplane parts built in the United States for Great Britain's Royal Air Force. She tested and inspected engines and engine parts in Curtiss training planes until the end of the war.

Before leaving her job, she bought a damaged Canuck, a Canadian training plane that was similar to the US Jenny. She shipped it home and put it in her parents' backyard. Airplanes were still rare in Iowa, and a plane in a backyard received extra attention. People kept stopping by to see what this young woman wanted with a wrecked airplane.

The truth was that she was rebuilding it, and she planned to fly it. The backyard had its uses, but there was no way she could take off from 828 Wilson Avenue in Ames, Iowa. After rebuilding the plane to her satisfaction, she began dismantling it so that she could move it to a pasture next to the Iowa State College campus. After reassembling the Canuck, she made her first solo flight.

US Jenny

Many airplanes have been designed since the beginning of aviation. Some have been successes, and others faded into obscurity. One of the earliest successes was the Curtiss JN-4D, designed by Glenn Curtiss and B. Douglas Thomas. It was a sturdy, open-cockpit propeller airplane used to train American and British pilots in World War I. More than 9,000 of these planes were manufactured. After the war, the Curtiss Aeroplane and Motor Company bought many back to refurbish and sell to civilian pilots. Others bought surplus Jennys from the federal government for as little as $200. Jennys were a favorite of barnstormers and were the first planes used for mail flights.

The US government was still recovering from World War I and didn't have the manpower to focus on the relatively new aviation industry. Neta and others like her received licenses for training and pleasure flights but weren't supposed to take passengers with them. Neta erased the *n* in "none" on her license to leave "one" as the number of passengers she could take. Because her Canuck was a biplane, only two people fit anyway—she and a passenger.

Neta began making money by barnstorming in the Midwest and charging people $15 for each 15-minute ride. She later inked a contract in the town where she was born to give two flights daily for three days. She received $1,000 for the six flights.

But Neta Snook didn't feel like a real pilot until she received her international license from the FAI. As soon as she had that

Barnstorming

Before there were stunt pilots, there were barnstormers. Early pilots, particularly those who had flown in World War I, had few options to make a living with flying. They found out that they could entertain audiences with aerial tricks and stunts. A barnstormer would attract locals in rural areas with aerobatics: diving, spins, barrel rolls, and the loop-the-loop. Some shows included aerialists who might perform wing walking, plane transfers, or trick parachuting. Sometimes a pilot would drop flyers on a town announcing a time and location. After watching the show, people in the audience would pay anywhere from one to five dollars for a ride. Some shows included more than one plane, and the event would become a sort of flying circus. Many famous aviators got their start in barnstorming, including Bessie Coleman, Charles Lindbergh, and Pancho Barnes (another woman pilot).

little blue book with her photo and license number, she decided it was time for a change. Iowa winters limited her flying, so she moved to where she could fly year-round: California.

After arriving, she got a job running a commercial airfield—Kinner Field in Los Angeles—and became the first woman to operate a commercial aviation business. She did a little of everything: took passengers for rides, tested new airplanes, towed aerial advertisements, and gave flight instructions.

In early 1921, a woman about Neta's age wearing a well-cut brown suit approached her. With a scarf around her neck and her gloves in her hands, the confident woman reminded Neta of the "cultured young ladies" back home in a private girls school. The woman introduced herself as Amelia Earhart, and she had a question for Neta: "Will you teach me to fly?"

Neta received 75 cents per minute for teaching Amelia Earhart to fly the Canuck she had built. Six months later, Amelia bought a Kinner Airster, a plane that Neta had tested for designer Bert Kinner. By now, the two women were also friends, and Neta stopped charging for lessons. Neta was concerned about Amelia flying the Kinner, a lighter plane that was harder to control. But Amelia was determined. On her first and only lesson with the Kinner, Amelia crashed it. Neither woman was hurt, but it took time to repair the airplane.

Neta married her boyfriend, William Southern, in 1921, and she wanted a baby. Early airplanes were dangerous, and many people died in the early days of aviation. Neta felt like she had to make a choice between flying and being a mother. Being a mother won. She traded her Canuck and lessons to fly it in August 1922 for a house and lot in Manhattan Beach and a $500 Liberty Bond. After the lessons, she never flew again. She didn't even ride in an airplane for 55 more years. But she did have a son, William Curtiss Southern, named after his father and aviator Glenn Curtiss.

Many years passed before Neta began lecturing and writing about her life as an early American aviator. Everyone wanted to meet the woman who taught Amelia Earhart to fly.

LEARN MORE

I Taught Amelia to Fly by Neta Snook Southern (Vantage Press, 1974)

"Neta Snook" on Ames Historical Society website, www
.ameshistoricalsociety.org/exhibits/snook.htm

"Neta Snook: Determined to Fly" on Iowa Pathways website (Iowa Public Television), www.iptv.org/iowapathways
/mypath.cfm?ounid=ob_000185

PART II

The Golden Age of Flight

omen like Bessie Coleman and Harriet Quimby may have demonstrated that women were capable of flying, but the barriers to flying refused to fall. Flying was not considered a ladylike activity. Many women had trouble finding people to give them lessons; others had trouble getting their pilot's licenses. Persistence was the key, and during the late 1920s it was beginning to pay off as more and more women took to the air.

Flying was expensive—both the lessons and the cost of airplanes—so it's no coincidence that many women pilots came from families with money. In 1928, a pilot's license cost $500. This was at a time when the average person's yearly income was $800.

Other women, such as Bobbi Trout, earned their way from the beginning. Still, flying was too expensive to be a hobby for most people. Some paid for aviation through exhibition flying or barnstorming. Some companies sponsored women who participated in races or set records. The companies' logos were featured on these pilots' planes.

Flying started as entertainment. At first, spectators were thrilled just to see people in the air. But as the number of pilots increased, air races became the way to draw crowds. Air races were the sports event of the day, attracting crowds of up to 150,000.

Then, on August 18, 1929, Charles Lindbergh crossed the Atlantic. For the next several years, records were being set and broken quickly as pilots of both sexes pushed the limits of aviation.

A strong string of firsts by women pilots took place in the 1920s and 1930s. Anne Morrow Lindbergh, the first US woman glider pilot, received the National Geographic Society's Hubbard Medal in 1934. She was the first female recipient, receiving the recognition for 40,000 miles (64,000 kilometers) of exploratory flying over five continents with her husband, famed aviator Charles Lindbergh.

Around the time Lindbergh went up, approximately 9,215 pilots were licensed, yet less than 1 percent of them were women. Many of those women pilots performed at exhibitions and set records. They weren't allowed to enter competitions, such as the National Air Race, because men decided those races were too dangerous for women. Amelia Earhart and other female pilots began talking about holding an air race for women only.

The first women's air race was the National Women's Air Derby. And it almost didn't get off the ground. Scheduled for 1929, the derby was a struggle to set up because most people still believed that women had no business flying airplanes, much less racing them. The National Air Race Committee felt that the 2,700-mile (4,350 kilometers) distance was too far and the hazards—including flying over the Rocky Mountains—were too great. They suggested a starting location of Omaha, Nebraska, instead of California.

Headlines and editorials from newspapers shouted that the race should be stopped. Threats of sabotage were made, but the women persevered. Amelia Earhart, already a nationally known figure, telegraphed the committee repeatedly about the conditions. When the committee tried to impose a rule that all the women must carry a male navigator or mechanic onboard, the women refused to fly. According to Louise Thaden, "To us the successful completion of the Derby was of more import than life or death."

Finally, the details were worked out, and the decision was made: 20 women would race from Santa Monica, California, to Cleveland, Ohio, on August 18, 1929. Pilots ranged from the famous—Amelia Earhart and Ruth Elder, who had made her living by flying in films—to the unknown, such as Neva Paris, Mary Haizlip, Opal Kunz, Mary von Mach, Vera Dawn Walker, Edith Foltz, and Jessie Keith-Miller.

The airplanes were lined up on Clover Field in Santa Monica by 1:30 PM with the temperatures approaching the 90s. Humorist Will Rogers, an advocate of aviation, was the starter. He called the pilots "petticoat pilots and flying flappers" and nicknamed the race the Powder Puff Derby, a name that stuck. At 2 PM, the pistol sounded, and they were off.

The eight-day race had a planned destination for each day: San Bernardino, Phoenix, El Paso, Fort Worth, Kansas City, Columbus, and more. The approximate distance was 310 miles (500 kilometers) during the daytime hours. Each contestant had a Rand McNally road map. Pilots also had emergency supplies in case of a crash: drinking water, milk tablets, and beef jerky.

Several contestants experienced problems, including Blanche Noyes and Pancho Barnes. Ruth Elder crashed. Thea Rasche, Claire Fahy, and a few others stated that someone had sabotaged their airplanes. Margaret Perry had to stop in the middle of the race to be hospitalized with typhoid fever. Marvel Crosson fatally crashed east of Yuma.

Fourteen contestants finished. The race was a success and was soon held each year. Women were eventually allowed to compete against men in races such as the Bendix. But for many of the women, the Women's Air Derby allowed them to meet others who shared the same love of flying. They formed friendships with people who really understood what it was like to be a female pilot.

Amelia Earhart, Louise Thaden, and others began talking about formally organizing a women's pilot organization. On November 2, 1929, 26 women gathered in a hangar at Curtiss Field in Valley Stream, Long Island, New York, to organize. A wheeled toolbox wagon held the tea that was served. The women decided the organization would be open to any licensed woman pilot and the function of the group would be "good fellowship, jobs, and a central office and files on women in aviation." The *New York Times* mentioned the meeting with the comments, "The women are going to organize. We don't know what for." Invitations went out to the 117 licensed women pilots of 1929. Of that number, 99 signed up. The group adopted the name "The Ninety-Nines" and voted Amelia Earhart as its first president.

The number of women pilots continued to grow after the formation of the Ninety-Nines. Two hundred women were licensed as pilots by 1930. In just five years, the number grew to almost 800.

The Ninety-Nines continues today as the largest women pilots' organization in the world. Its headquarters is in Oklahoma City, where the Ninety-Nines Museum of Women Pilots showcases the history of women in aviation. The Ninety-Nines also operates the Amelia Earhart Birthplace Museum in Atchison, Kansas.

Additionally, the organization also develops, organizes, and participates in air races. The Women's Air Derby became the

All-Woman Transcontinental Air Race and was held annually for 30 years. The Air Race Classic, which continues to be held today, is similar to the Women's Air Derby but has a different course every year. There was also an All Women's International Air Race, also called the Angel Derby. Other races have included the Palms to Pines Air Race, New England Air Race, and Michigan Small Race.

≣ AMELIA EARHART ≣

The Most Famous Female
Aviator in the World

As HER 40TH BIRTHDAY approached, Amelia Earhart was ready for the ultimate challenge: flying around the world. Her first attempt in March 1937 ended on the second leg of her journey. Although she had made it from Oakland, California, to Hawaii, she crashed her Lockheed Electra upon takeoff from Honolulu's Luke Field. The crash meant almost a two-month delay for her airplane to be repaired. The delay also meant a change in weather patterns and air currents. Instead of an equatorial trip going from east to west, she was going to have to reverse her route and go west to east.

Amelia took off from Oakland, California, on May 20, 1937, with Fred Noonan as her navigator. Stops for refueling, rest, and publicity purposes would be part of the entire trip. Their last stop in the continental United States was Miami; then they left for Puerto Rico on June 1. They followed the northeast coast of South America before crossing the Atlantic for Dakar, Senegal, in Africa.

On June 10, Amelia and her navigator crossed Africa, a trip that made her a little nervous. What if they crashed and were lost in the jungle? But they experienced no problems and departed Africa on June 15, headed for Pakistan. They followed the southern edge of Asia, landing in Australia on June 28. The next day, they reached Lae, New Guinea. They had flown 22,000 miles (35,400 kilometers) and had only 7,000 more miles (11,300 kilometers) to go, but that distance involved the longest over-water flights. In fact, their next stop was on Howland Island, 2,556 miles (4,113 kilometers) away.

Less than a mile wide and two miles long, the tiny How-land Island would be easy to miss if they were off course. The US government helped by building a runway and would have ships positioned off shore of the island. Maps in 1937 weren't as accurate as today's maps, and there was no satellite or GPS to follow. In fact, Noonan mainly navigated by looking at the stars and the sun.

On July 2, 1937, Amelia Earhart and Fred Noonan took off for Howland Island. The pair had unloaded everything from the plane that they didn't absolutely need so they could carry extra fuel.

When Amelia checked in with a Coast Guard ship, the *Itasca*, she reported cloudy weather. Radio transmissions were faint and filled with static. Amelia wasn't responding to their questions. The Itasca realized that Amelia couldn't hear them. Something was wrong with her radio.

"We must be on you, but we cannot see you. Fuel is running low. Been unable to reach you by radio. We are flying at 1,000 feet," Amelia transmitted. About an hour later, she said, "We are on the line of position 156-137. We are running north and south." That was the last anyone heard from Amelia Earhart.

———•———

Amelia had always had a sense of adventure. Born on July 24, 1897, in Atchison, Kansas, she climbed trees, raced her sled down hills, and orchestrated imaginative pretend trips for herself, her sister, and other children. From her well-off grandparents, whom she often stayed with as a child, she learned about the wonder of books and education. She was devastated when they died within months of each other in 1911.

Amelia's parents loved and encouraged her, but there were problems at home because of her father's alcoholism. Edwin Earhart, a railroad attorney, had difficulty holding onto a job because of his drinking. The Earharts moved to Des Moines, Iowa, when Amelia was in seventh grade and continued to move frequently as her father lost jobs. In all, Amelia attended six high schools, but she still managed to graduate on time.

When Amelia left to attend Columbia University, she didn't know exactly what she wanted to do, but she knew it should be important. She was drawn to stories of successful women and had a scrapbook about them that she kept during her childhood.

While visiting her sister in Toronto during World War I, Amelia worked as a nurse's aide at a military hospital. One day, she and a friend attended a stunt-flying exhibition. She had seen an airplane before, at the state fair when she was 10 years old, and hadn't been impressed. This time, however, she was. The pilot flew his plane toward Amelia to tease and frighten her a little. He expected her scream and run out of the way, but she faced the plane as if daring the pilot to hit her.

Amelia left school and moved to California in 1923 to live with her parents. She and her father often attended air shows, and on December 28, 1920, she experienced her first flight. In that moment, she knew she had to fly.

Two weeks later, she approached Neta Snook and started flying lessons. Amelia worked as a clerk for the telephone company and as a photographer to pay for those lessons. With her mother's financial help, Amelia bought a bright yellow Kinner Airster. She named it *Canary* and soon set a women's altitude record of 14,000 feet (4,270 meters).

On May 16, 1923, Amelia became the 16th woman in the world to earn a pilot's license from the FAI. But money was limited, especially after her parents' divorce. Amelia sold her airplane and drove her mother from California to Massachusetts, where they moved in with Amelia's sister, Muriel. Amelia worked with immigrant families as a social worker at Denison House in Boston. Her free time was spent at the airport trying to get flying time.

In spring of 1928, she received a call from George Putnam, a publisher and publicist, looking for a woman to be the first female to fly over the Atlantic Ocean. There was a catch, though. She wouldn't be piloting the airplane; she would fly as a passenger. Still, the flight provided an opportunity to make the trip and profit from it by writing about her experiences.

On June 17, 1928, Amelia took off from Newfoundland with pilots Wilmer Stultz and Lou Gordon. In 20 hours and 40 minutes, they landed in Wales. She wrote a book about the experience called *20 Hrs., 40 Min.* Although Amelia was just a passenger, all the attention was focused on her, which she found ridiculous. However, it allowed her to spend all her time focused on aviation—flying, writing, and speaking about it.

One of Amelia's first competitions was the Women's Air Derby, a race she helped organize. She placed third. She also became the first woman to fly an autogiro, a flying machine that looks like a cross between a helicopter and an airplane. In 1931, a chewing-gum company called Beechnut paid her to tour the country in an autogiro. She set an altitude record of 18,415 feet (5,617 meters) in the machine but also experienced three crashes.

Amelia was a stylish figure in the brown breeches and brown leather jacket that she preferred. Years before, she began gradually cutting her hair until she was satisfied with the short style. The newspapers often called her "Lady Lindy" after the famed aviator Charles Lindbergh, the first man to fly solo nonstop across the Atlantic. Amelia hated the name and much preferred to be called "AE." Yet the most famous male and female aviators of the day did share a resemblance to each other with their slim builds and similar facial features.

The nickname spurred her to consider an idea she had carried around since the passenger flight that made her famous. What if she flew across the Atlantic—this time as a pilot? She would do it the same way Lindbergh had, solo and nonstop. Many men had tried and failed, some losing their lives in the process. One other woman, Ruth Nichols, had tried and failed in 1931.

On May 20, 1932, Amelia took off from Harbour Grace, Newfoundland, in Canada in a red-and-gold Lockheed Vega 5B. It was exactly five years after Lindbergh had taken his historic flight. The 2,026-mile (3,260 kilometers) trip was challenging. She had to deal with a damaged exhaust manifold that occasionally caused flames to shoot out from the vent. Ice formed on her wings if she flew too high, and she risked crashing into the cold ocean water if she flew too low. About 15 hours later, she landed in a farmer's backyard in Londonderry, Northern Ireland. She greeted the surprised farmer with, "Hello, I'm Amelia Earhart."

Amelia wasn't the best pilot of her generation, but she was one of the most courageous. As the first woman and second person in the world to fly solo across the Atlantic Ocean, Amelia became even more famous. More important to her, she proved that a woman could pilot an airplane just as well as a man.

Months later, Amelia was setting distance and speed records in transcontinental flights. She also made a second, much better trip across the Atlantic and became the first person to cross the Atlantic twice. After conquering the Atlantic, she turned her sights on the Pacific, becoming the first person to fly solo from

The First Woman to Fly Around the World

Twenty-seven years would go by before another woman would accomplish what Amelia tried: a flight around the world. That woman was Geraldine Mock, nicknamed "the Flying Housewife" by the media. More commonly known as Jerrie, she flew a single-engine Cessna 180 called the *Spirit of Columbus* on her historic flight.

Married to a pilot, Jerrie took flight lessons at the age of 37 and enjoyed flying with her husband. She took off on her trip on March 19, 1964, with only 750 flight hours logged. She faced hazardous weather and problems with the brakes and radio. Jerrie even accidently landed on a secret military base in Egypt. She completed her journey of 23,103 miles (37,173 kilometers) in 29 days, 11 hours, and 59 minutes. Jerrie went on to set many speed records over the next five years.

Hawaii to California, which she did on January 11–12, 1935. The trip was almost 400 miles (640 kilometers) farther than the flight across the Atlantic.

Throughout her life, Amelia supported other women and encouraged them to follow their dreams, whether they wanted to fly or do something else. As aviation editor at *Cosmopolitan* magazine, she recommended to readers that they learn to fly. To mothers, she advised, "Let your daughters fly."

In 1935, Amelia became a visiting consultant at Purdue University, speaking on women's career opportunities. Purdue, supportive of her flying, created the Amelia Earhart Fund for Aeronautical Research and purchased a twin-engine Lockheed 10-E Electra, which would become a "flying laboratory." This plane, which she took on her world trip, was equipped with the latest in aviation technology, including two 500-horsepower engines and communication equipment.

The search for Amelia and her navigator lasted 17 days, covering 250,000 square miles (650,000 square kilometers) at a cost of $4 million. No trace of them or the Lockheed Electra could be found. The government assumed the two were lost at sea.

People had theories about what had happened to Amelia and Fred, of course: They were spies and had completed their mission. They were living on an island. They had adopted new names and moved to another country. They had been captured and killed by the Japanese, who would later bomb Pearl Harbor and lead the United States into World War II.

More than 75 years later, no one is certain of Amelia's fate. Most experts now believe that her receiving antenna broke upon takeoff from New Guinea, which would explain why she couldn't hear transmissions from the US Navy and Coast Guard. Her disappearance remains one of the greatest unsolved mysteries of the 20th century.

Will the Amelia Earhart Mystery Finally Be Solved?

Since Amelia's disappearance in the Pacific, many people have speculated about what her last minutes, hours, and days were like. One group investigating more than 75 years later is the International Group for Historic Aircraft Recovery (TIGHAR). Its members believe that Amelia and her navigator were forced to find another location to land because of their low fuel supply. The theory, based on digital analysis of the radio signals, is that they landed on the coral reef of Gardner Island, now known as Nikumaroro Island. This is approximately 300 miles (480 kilometers) southeast of Howland Island. Ocean tides would have eventually swept the Lockheed Electra into the ocean, promptly sinking it.

On the 75th anniversary of Amelia's disappearance, the TIGHAR's Niku VII expedition left from Hawaii to search for the Lockheed Electra in the waters around Nikumaroro Island with high-tech equipment. The researchers at TIGHAR hoped to finally locate Amelia Earhart's airplane and perhaps answer some questions about her disappearance. After a 26-day expedition with sonar detection and high-definition, TIGHAR came up empty-handed. The mystery of Ameila Earhart's fate continues.

"If I should bop off, it'll be doing the thing that I've always most wanted to do," she told her friend and fellow pilot Louise Thaden before her epic journey.

LEARN MORE

Amelia Earhart Birthplace Museum, www.ameliaearhart museum.org

Amelia Earhart Official Site, www.ameliaearhart.com

"The Earhart Project" on the International Group for Historical Aircraft Recovery website, http://tighar.org

The Fun of It: Random Records of My Own Flying and of Women in Aviation by Amelia Earhart (Kessinger Publishing, 2010)

Last Flight by Amelia Earhart (Random House, reprinted 1999)

Letters from Amelia: An Intimate Portrait of Amelia Earhart by Amelia Earhart and Jean L. Backus (Beacon Press, 1982)

20 Hrs., 40 Min.: Our Flight in the Friendship by Amelia Earhart (National Geographic, reprinted 2003)

≣ LOUISE THADEN ≣
Women's Air Derby Winner

IN THE 1930S, THE BENDIX Transcontinental Air Race from Cleveland to Los Angeles (which, for two years, started in New York) was considered the top prize for any pilot, male or female. The problem was that the annual race didn't allow women to race. The death of a female pilot in the 1933 Frank Phillips Trophy Race disturbed aviation's establishment, which insisted on banning women from competition. But the increasing numbers of determined women aviators made this ban difficult to keep.

Then, in the fifth year of the Bendix, the ban was lifted, and Amelia Earhart took fifth place. The following year, 1936, Amelia was joined in the quest by Laura Ingalls and Louise Thaden, with Blanche Noyes as copilot. The planes took off from New York on September 4, 1936. Louise and Blanche flew a Beechcraft

C17R Staggerwing biplane, a new plane from Beechcraft that was built more aerodynamically, with the lower wing staggered in front of the upper wing.

Louise and Blanche discovered almost immediately that their radio was out. They had no idea what position they were in as they flew across country. But Louise was soon forced to forget about the lack of communication: after they reached Albuquerque, strong headwinds and turbulence bounced their plane around and demanded all their attention.

When Louise and Blanche landed in Los Angeles, exhausted, they assumed they were in last place. Louise didn't even want to land; she wanted to keep flying. Then they goofed by coming across the finish line from the wrong direction. They had trouble seeing because of the afternoon sun and poor visibility due to a nearby forest fire. With everything that had gone wrong, they just wanted to hide, but their bright blue plane refused to fade into the background in front of the crowd of 15,000.

People had said that Louise and Blanche had about as much chance of winning as a "draft horse [had] of winning the Kentucky Derby." But, on the ground in Los Angeles, the director of the National Air Races approached the women and told them, "I'm afraid you've won the Bendix race." With no radio contact, they hadn't realized that they weren't last, let alone first.

Their win, at 14 hours and 55 minutes, meant Louise and Blanche received $7,000—$4,500 for placing first and a bonus of $2,500 for being the first women to finish. Laura Ingalls came in second place 45 minutes later.

It wasn't the first race Louise had won. In 1929, she flew a Travel Air B-4000 from Santa Monica, California, to Cleveland, Ohio, to win the first Women's Air Derby, better known as the Powder Puff Derby. Louise, the youngest of the contestants at age 23, beat favorites Amelia Earhart and Pancho Barnes with a

Blanche Noyes

A former actress, Blanche Noyes switched to flying when her husband, an airmail pilot, introduced her to it. He bought Blanche her first plane and taught her to fly. When she soloed on February 15, 1929, she found something she loved more than acting. Five months later, she had her license. A month after that, she flew in the National Women's Air Derby.

Blanche flew as a demonstration pilot and for corporations in the first half of the 1930s, but she switched gears when her husband died in a crash in 1935. One of the five women chosen by Phoebe Omlie for the Air Marking Program, Blanche devoted much of her time to air safety and was the only woman allowed to fly government aircraft for a while. She received the Commerce Department's Gold Medal for her work.

time of 20 hours, 2 minutes, and 2 seconds and an average speed of just less than 136 miles per hour.

Winning the first Women's Air Derby didn't come easily either. Louise experienced periods in her aircraft during which she was dizzy and her vision clouded. Soon after landing in Fort Worth, she fainted. It was determined that there was a problem with the exhaust system—Louise had been breathing in carbon monoxide. Mechanics installed a pipe that would bring clean air into the plane, and Louise had to finish the race with her nose to the pipe.

Louise McPhetridge was born in Bentonville, Arkansas, on November 12, 1905, to Edna and Roy McPhetridge. Louise grew up on a farm, and her father, a traveling salesman, taught her to hunt, fish, and fix a car. She developed an interest in flying early on. When Louise was five years old, she begged for five dollars to buy a ride from a barnstormer. That amount allowed her only five minutes of flying time, but it was enough.

After graduating from high school, Louise attended the University of Arkansas. She didn't know what she wanted to do. She started as a journalism major, later changing to physical education. Instead of returning for a fourth year of college, Louise moved to Wichita, Kansas, to work as a sales clerk for a coal company. Her employer was on the board of Travel Air. Louise spent as much time as she could at the airfield, until Walter Beech, the owner of Travel Air, offered her a sales job in Oakland, California. The best part of her new job was that flying lessons were part of the benefits package.

The year 1928 was a busy one for Louise. She earned her pilot's license, signed by Orville Wright, in May. Two months later, she married Herbert von Thaden, a US Army pilot and aeronautical engineer. By the end of the year, she set one of many records: a women's altitude record, which she clinched at 20,260 feet (6,179 meters). Within four months, she also held women's endurance and speed records and was the only woman to hold all three records at the same time.

After her 1929 Women's Air Derby win, Louise, Amelia Earhart, and Ruth Nichols established the Ninety-Nines. Louise served as treasurer and vice president in the group's early years.

Working as the public relations director of Pittsburgh Aviation Industries, Louise took every opportunity to publicize aviation and even wrote articles about it. She became director of the

Women's Division of the Penn School of Aeronautics—the first flight school to have a women's division—in 1930.

But her aviation records, such as a refueling endurance record, drew the most attention. Louise flew over Long Island, New York, from August 14 to 22, 1932, with Frances Marsalis to establish a 196-hour refueling endurance record. Fellow aviator Viola Gentry organized food and supplies. Live radio broadcasts from their Curtiss Thrush biplane generated publicity. They went 74 hours longer than the previous endurance record, which had been set by Bobbi Trout and Edna May Cooper. Their long ride wasn't a comfortable one. They had stripped out the extra seat, so they brought an air mattress for naps—but it was punctured during the second day.

In 1934, Louise's friend, fellow pilot Phoebe Omlie, convinced Louise to work with her on the Air Marking Program. Phoebe had convinced the government that using paint or bricks on the roofs of tall buildings or hillsides to identify airports and towns would help pilots navigate from the air. The Bureau of Air Commerce put Phoebe in charge. Louise enjoyed the work. Phoebe appointed her to be in charge of the western part of the United States. At least 13,000 markers were created throughout the country.

Soon after Louise's Bendix win, she received the Harmon Trophy for outstanding aviation. A year later, she took a break from flying to spend time with her family, including her two young children, Bill and Pat. During this time, she also wrote a book about her adventures, *High, Wide, and Frightened*.

During World War II, Louise joined the Civil Air Patrol, soon rising to the rank of lieutenant colonel and working with her old friend Ruth Nichols on Relief Wings.

Louise last raced with her daughter in the 1950 International Women's Air Race from Montreal, Canada, to West Palm Beach,

Florida, for a fifth-place finish. A year later, her hometown of
Bentonville renamed its airport Louise M. Thaden Field.

LEARN MORE

High, Wide, and Frightened by Louise Thaden and Patty
Wagstaff (University of Arkansas Press, reprinted
2004)

"Louise McPhetridge Thaden (1905–1979)" on
Encyclopedia of Arkansas History and Culture website,
http://encyclopediaofarkansas.net/encyclopedia/entry
-detail.aspx?search=1&entryID=30

"Louise Thaden" on National Aviation Hall of Fame website,
www.nationalaviation.org/thaden-louise/

≣ BOBBI TROUT ≣

From Service Station to Airfield

Twelve-year-old Evelyn "Bobbi" Trout was outside one day when she heard a loud noise. Looking up, she saw an airplane, the first she had ever seen. She kept it in her sight as long as she could. When the airplane was gone, she grinned and said, "I'm going to fly airplanes when I grow up."

———•———

Born in Greenup, Illinois, on January 7, 1906, Evelyn Trout preferred fixing things to cooking and sewing. When she was 14, she and her parents moved to Los Angeles. Mrs. Trout did her best to get her daughter to dress like girls did in the 1920s, but she threw up her hands in defeat when Bobbi came home one day with a very short hairstyle called a bob. Bobbi had seen it on movie star Irene Castle. That's when Evelyn became "Bobbi."

Bobbi went to school and thought about becoming an architect. She enjoyed competing in sports; she was best at swimming. At home, money was often tight, particularly when her father was in charge of it. He was known to have schemes that didn't work. He also disappeared from time to time. Bobbi must have inherited her mother's sense of business, because the two owned and operated a successful gas station, the Radio Service Station. Her mother took care of the money, while Bobbi served the customers. Music and comedy shows played over the radio speakers. Customers would listen while Bobbi filled up their cars with gasoline and washed their windows.

When Bobbi started talking about airplanes, her eyes lit up. One of the customers, W. E. "Tommy" Thomas, just happened to have a Curtiss Jenny airplane. He offered 16-year-old Bobbi a ride. That first flight was everything she had hoped it would be.

Bobbi began saving her money for flying lessons. When she had saved $2,500, she approached Burdett Fuller, who ran an aviation school. On the first day of 1928, Bobbi Trout began learning to fly. It wasn't all fun. One day, she worked with a young flight instructor on forced landings. He insisted that she make a three-quarter turn and land. She told him the elevation was too low. He disagreed and decided he would show this opinionated girl what a male pilot could do. He crashed the Jenny. It was her first and last lesson with this pilot.

Four months later, Bobbi soloed; she got her license two weeks after that. Bobbi's mother then bought her an International K-6, a four-place biplane. Bobbi became the fifth woman in America to obtain a transport license, which she did in 1930, two years after becoming a licensed pilot.

Bobbi knew she had to have a sponsor if she wanted to make a living from flying. Sunset Oil Company said it would provide her with free fuel and oil if she would allow its painted logo on her airplane. (Sunset Oil would be the first of many sponsors; Bobbi even flew Mickey Mouse around for Walt Disney.)

One day, a man approached her after she landed the Jenny. His name was R. O. Bone. He said, "I need someone to demonstrate my new airplane. Are you interested? I'll give you $35 a week."

"When do I start?" Bobbi asked.

The plane was the Golden Eagle, an experimental airplane with a LeBlond 60-horsepower engine designed by Mark Campbell. Bobbi won her first race in it. On January 2, 1929, she took it up before dawn. She returned 12 hours and 11 minutes later, making her first night landing. Even more important, she had set a women's solo endurance record.

Then, later that month, Elinor Smith broke Bobbi's record. So Bobbi went up again just over a month after that; she lasted five hours longer than Smith and reclaimed the record. When she landed, she got a surprise: cameras and movie stars were waiting for her, including one of the most popular men in America, Will Rogers.

Airplanes were getting more powerful, and Bobbi's was just too small and light. By the summer of 1929, she moved up to a 90-horsepower Golden Eagle Chief. When she broke 15,200 feet (4,636 meters), she added an altitude record to her other achievements.

She had been talking to other pilots, such as Louise Thaden and Elinor Smith, about a woman's refueling endurance flight. But before that could happen, it was time for the first Women's Air Derby, a transcontinental race in which she would fly Bone's newest plane: the 90-horsepower Golden Eagle Chief, a high-wing monoplane.

On August 18, 1929, Bobbi joined 19 other licensed female pilots at Clover Field in Santa Monica, California. She drew the fifth start. As the flag went down, she made an effortless takeoff. On the second day, her engine stopped while she was in flight. When making an emergency landing six miles from the Yuma Airport, she flipped over. Damage to the plane took three days to repair. However, even after waiting for repairs, she managed to catch up with many of the pilots near Kansas City. She hadn't been the only one with problems.

Her plane suffered more engine problems, but this time she made her own repairs. She figured she was out of the race, but she pushed on and eventually finished. Bobbi Trout never quit.

After the derby, Bobbi focused on the women's refueling endurance flight with Elinor Smith. Promoter Jack Sherrill had arranged for them to use a Sunbeam biplane. They flipped a coin to determine who would fly first. Elinor won.

They took off on November 25, 1929. The two pilots planned to alternate flying and sleeping in four-hour shifts. Bobbi could rest, but only after she performed necessary jobs. And refueling wasn't the only task: Engine oil needed to be changed daily, and the rocker arms needed to be greased. Fuel had to be pumped from the cabin tank to the fuel tank, an exhausting job that took a lot of arm strength. Supplies and fuel came courtesy of a rope, which was lowered from another airplane. Provisions were lowered in a bag. The other plane then lowered a pipe for fueling. Bobbi would catch the bag and rope. The nozzle was then be secured to a port in the cabin fuel tanks. From there, 180 gallons (680 liters) of fuel were hand-pumped from the bigger tanks to the plane's smaller tank.

All went well on the first attempt until the planes drifted apart, jerking the gas line out and soaking Bobbi with gasoline. She also swallowed some of it. Elinor quickly landed, and Bobbi was rushed to the hospital.

They took off again on November 27, 1929. The first two days went well, but on the third day, Bobbi noticed black smoke coming from the exhaust of the supply plane above them. Where there's smoke, there's often fire—and gasoline is highly flammable. Bobbi pulled the hose out quickly, while Elinor moved their plane away from the supply plane. The supply plane had to make a forced landing. There would be no more refueling.

Bobbi and Elinor remained in the air as long as their fuel lasted. They landed after 42 hours and 3.5 minutes. They were the first all-woman refueling endurance flight.

Bobbi went on to break that refueling record with actress and aviator Edna May Cooper on January 4, 1931. She even celebrated her 25th birthday in the air with birthday cake sent up by a friend. On day three of that flight, their engine began to cough and spit oil. When they were no longer able to maintain altitude, they landed. They had used 1,138 gallons (4,307 liters) of fuel. Their official time in the air was 122 hours and 50 minutes.

The refueling endurance flight brought Bobbi more acclaim, including the Fédération Aéronautique Internationale Medallion from the FAI. She also became one of three aviators to receive the Aviation Cross from King Carol II of Romania. The other two recipients were Amelia Earhart and Charles Lindbergh.

When the Great Depression arrived, Bobbi worked as a flight instructor for a while before joining fellow pilot Pancho Barnes in the Women's Air Reserve, which would allow them to help in catastrophes. The organization flew in medical personnel and supplies to disaster sites. Bobbi received training in first aid, navigation, and military maneuvers.

World War II dried up many flying jobs, but Bobbi learned that aircraft manufacturers were just throwing away rivets because it was too expensive to pay people to sort them. Metal was even more precious during wartime, so Bobbi invented a machine to sort airplane rivets during manufacturing. The rivet-sorting machine saved unused rivets that fell to the ground during the manufacturing process. Her business, the Aero Reclaiming Company, was successful, and she sold it three years later. She then developed deburring equipment to smooth out the edges of machined metal. Because of her inventions, Bobbi was awarded a certificate of achievement from Inventors Workshop International.

Bobbi last piloted an airplane in 1984. She wore many different hats after her golden days of flying: commercial photographer, real estate broker, offset printer, and life insurance and mutual fund salesperson. When Bobbi Trout died at 97 on January 24, 2003, she was the last of the surviving participants of the 1929 Women's Air Derby.

LEARN MORE

"Bobbi Evelyn Trout" on Ninety-Nines International Organization of Women Pilots website, www.ninety-nines.org/index.cfm/bobbi_trout.htm

Bobbi Trout website, www.bobbitrout.com

Powder Puff Derby of 1929: The True Story of the First Women's Cross-Country Air Race by Gene Nora Jessen (Sourcebooks, 2002)

≣ ELINOR SMITH ≣

The Flying Flapper of Freeport

ON A BRIGHT, CLEAR OCTOBER Sunday, a 17-year-old girl with a two-month-old pilot's license was getting ready to take a flight. But this particular endeavor was unique. It could result in her losing her license—or her life. The year was 1928, and she was about to fly under New York City's four bridges, a feat never before tried.

As she was waiting to climb in her plane, she tensed when someone tapped her shoulder. Was it the police or perhaps the newsmen who had dared her to attempt this feat? She turned and saw a kind, handsome face, one known throughout the world: Charles Lindbergh.

"Good luck, kid. Remember to keep your nose down in the turns," Lindbergh said, grinning.

Shaking her head in amazement, Elinor Smith watched one of her heroes walk off. Imagine. Charles Lindbergh, who had made his famous trip from New York to Paris around the time of her first solo, had come to see her make this historic flight.

She took off in her father's Waco 9 biplane. The view of Long Island Sound and the Atlantic Ocean was incredible. In her autobiography, she wrote, "And the clouds on that particular day had just broken open so there were these shafts of light coming down and lighting up this whole landscape in various greens and yellows."

New York City is a city surrounded by water—not only the Atlantic Ocean, but also the Hudson and East Rivers. Manhattan, one of the city's five boroughs, is actually an island. Four bridges provide a way across the East River into Manhattan. The Brooklyn, Manhattan, and Williamsburg Bridges connect Brooklyn and Manhattan. The Queensboro Bridge, also known as the 59th Street Bridge, connects Manhattan to Queens. During her flight, Elinor had to dodge a few ocean liners, but she was successful.

Eight days later, she was summoned to the mayor's office. Elinor couldn't stop shaking. What if mayor Jimmy Walker took away her license? Never let her fly again? She just wouldn't be able to stand it.

The mayor looked at the girl standing in front of him and sighed. Who would have thought that this five-foot, three-inch girl could raise so much havoc in his city?

He began, "You're suspended . . ." and then paused as he heard her gasp. In a gentle voice, he continued, "You're suspended from flying for ten days, retroactive to the day of your flight. I believe that means two more days of not flying."

"Oh, thank you, Mayor Walker," Elinor said. She left the New York City mayor's office. She still had her pilot's license, and she had done something no other pilot had done. What would the Flying Flapper of Freeport, as the media called her, have thought if she had known that her record would still stand 85 years later?

———•———

Born on August 17, 1911, Elinor Smith grew up in Freeport, Long Island, New York. As the daughter of vaudeville performer Tom Smith, she grew up with supportive parents who encouraged her to challenge herself. She was taught that her gender shouldn't interfere with what she wanted to do.

One day when she was six years old, the family was driving along Merrick Road. The children screamed for Tom to stop when they saw a sign that read, AIRPLANE RIDES—$5 AND $10. Elinor's father talked to the pilot and then returned to get the children. After tying Elinor's blond braids together to keep them out of her face, he lifted her and her brother, Joe, into the second seat, strapping them in together in the Farman pusher biplane.

The ride marked the beginning of Elinor's love of flying. She was taking lessons by age 10 and soloing at 15. Soon after her first solo flight, she set an unofficial women's altitude record of 11,874 feet (3,619 meters).

When she earned her pilot's license, signed by Orville Wright, she was the youngest pilot the FAI had seen yet. At 18, she was granted a transport pilot's license, the first person in the United States to receive one. "I had been brought up to think that anyone could do anything he or she put his or her mind to, so I was shocked to learn that the world had stereotypes it didn't want tampered with."

From 1929 to 1930, Elinor joined a cross-country tour as a demonstration pilot for an airplane manufacturer, Bellanca. She also flew for a group of parachutists to promote the Irvin Air

Chute Company. Women pilots were often limited to the lighter planes, but Elinor knew the size of the plane didn't matter. She flew the big six-passenger Bellanca, astounding the press that a 17-year-old female could do such a thing.

"Becoming a professional pilot was for me the most desirable goal in the world, and I was not going to allow age or sex to bar me from it," she recalled about that time.

Records were being set almost daily. Elinor decided she would set the first women's endurance records. Viola Gentry beat her to it by flying for more than eight hours. Less than two weeks later, Bobbi Trout pushed that to 12 hours.

Elinor didn't let it bother her. She just beat them both with a flight time of 13 hours, 16 minutes, and 45 seconds. It was her first world record, set on January 31, 1929. She flew in an open-cockpit Bird biplane. Strong winds and fog surrounded her, and the temperature dropped. She had dressed warmly, but the temperature was below freezing. She was ready to land by 3:00 AM but had never landed at night—plus the visibility was poor. Nevertheless, she did it. And almost three months later, she nearly doubled her endurance time. Elinor, Bobbi, Viola, and Louise Thaden continued to take turns holding the women's endurance record for the next few years.

Elinor went on to set more records for endurance, altitude, and speed than anyone. Sometimes, she beat her own records. Together, she and Bobbi Trout became the first women pilots to refuel in the air successfully.

In 1930, Elinor was chosen by other pilots as the woman pilot of the year. Still a teenager, she was honored by the recognition. No doubt her women's altitude record of 27,418 feet (8,357 meters) earlier in the year had a lot to do with the award. A year later, at Roosevelt Field on Long Island, she added more than 5,000 feet (1,500 meters) to her altitude record.

Elinor made her mark on aviation in other ways as well. In addition to writing aviation articles for magazines and commentating for NBC radio, she was an advisor to the New York State Aviation Committee. She continued performing at air shows and as a movie stunt pilot.

Elinor met a New York politician and attorney, Patrick Sullivan, and in 1933, they married. When she became pregnant with her third child, she decided to quit flying to raise her family. She had four children in all.

Twenty-five years later, after her husband's death, Elinor returned to flying, now as a member of the Air Force Association. She thrilled at flying the T-33 jet trainer and the C-119 for paratrooper maneuvers. In 2000, Elinor was invited to fly the NASA Vertical Motion Simulator. She was successful, which came as no surprise to anyone who knew her. She became the oldest pilot to land a simulated shuttle and was delighted to have an all-female support crew.

LEARN MORE

Aviatrix by Elinor Smith (Thorndike Press, reprinted 1982)

"Elinor Smith" on Cradle of Aviation Museum website, www.cradleofaviation.org/history/people/smith.html

"Elinor Smith: Born to Fly" on NASA website, www.nasa.gov/topics/people/features/elinor-smith.html

≣ EDNA GARDNER WHYTE ≣

Nothing Could Stop
Her from Flying

MANY EARLY WOMEN PILOTS had to fight to pursue their passion to fly. For some, the battle against discrimination and society's expectations was just too much to overcome. Others did fight it, every step of the way. Edna Gardner Whyte was one of those women. She was an exhibition flyer, a flight instructor, and a businesswoman in aviation.

———•———

Born on November 3, 1902, Edna had wanted to fly since she was a little girl. Unlike many early women pilots, Edna didn't have a privileged childhood. She spent her youth on a Minnesota farm, where the only speed she experienced came from riding horses.

Later, she would drive a Model T and see firsthand how fast it could go—and she even ended up rolling it over.

When Edna was seven, her family moved to Seattle, where her father got a job with the railroad. He was killed in a head-on collision within the year. Then her mother became ill from tuberculosis and was sent to a sanitarium. Edna and her brother and sister were split up and sent to live with different relatives. The rest of her childhood was spent moving from home to home.

When Edna grew up, she became a nurse. While in nurse's training, she had devoured articles about Katherine and Marjorie Stinson. The sisters were pilots who had been asked by president Woodrow Wilson to train pilots to fly in World War I. One of Edna's patients offered to take her up in his airplane. She wrote of the experience, "He showed me how to use the stick—nose up, nose down, nose sideways. We were following the roads, dirt and gravel back then, and I thought it was wonderful."

Edna found someone who agreed to teach her. She paid $35 per hour, half her monthly salary. When Edna went to test for her license in 1928, she received the highest grade on the written portion of the exam. But when it came time for her flight test, the government inspector refused to test her.

"But why?" she asked.

He said, "I've never tested a woman, and I don't know that I want to start now. Women don't belong in airplanes. That's a man's job."

Edna told the inspector how hard she had worked. She even cried. He relented, and she earned her license. The next year, when she joined the Navy Nurse Corps, she was stationed at Newport's naval hospital. In her free time, she flew, winning her first race in 1933. She also began teaching flying to others.

The Flying Stinsons

The Stinsons were a flying family of brothers and sisters. Eldest sister Katherine sold her family's piano to pay for flying lessons and became the fourth American woman to earn a license in 1912. Ironically, she wanted the flying lessons so that she could earn money for a music career. Katherine was very small in size and looked younger than her 21 years when she began performing in air exhibitions in the United States and Europe. She was nicknamed "the Flying School-girl." Katherine later became the first woman authorized to be an airmail pilot.

Marjorie Stinson followed in her older sister's footsteps, becoming the ninth American woman pilot to receive her license two years later. She soon became the only woman in the US Aviation Reserve Corps. Although she also was certified as an airmail carrier, her talents seemed to lie in flight instruction.

After hearing about Florence Klingensmith doing 68 consecutive loops, Edna decided to try aerobatics. She asked some male pilots how to do a loop.

"When you're up, drive toward the ground and build up speed. Then put your plane back over the top."

Edna's first attempt was memorable. Her engine stalled, plus everything that could come out of the plane did—and landed right on Edna. Thankfully, she had goggles on, as a lot of dirt and even a couple of dead mice rained upon her face. But Edna didn't quit. She kept trying and worked up to 38 loops.

In 1915, the Stinson family opened the Stinson School for Aviation at San Antonio's Kelly Field. They trained pilots for the US Army and Canada's Royal Flying Corps. Perhaps as a nod to Katherine's nickname, people began calling Marjorie "the Flying Schoolmarm" until 1918, when the school closed.

During World War I, Katherine participated in fundraising tours for the Red Cross and drove an ambulance in Europe. A bad case of influenza weakened her health and ended her aviation career. Marjorie changed careers in 1928 and became a draftsman for the Aeronautical Division of the US Navy.

Katherine Stinson.
Courtesy of Chicago Daily News negatives collection, Chicago History Museum

After transferring to the US Naval Hospital in Washington, DC, Edna entered an air race that offered $300 to the winner. Although she won the otherwise all-male race, she noticed the group of male officials huddled together. She figured they were trying to find a way to disqualify her. Two other pilots stepped up and told the judges that she had won fair and square. The race was advertised the next year with a sign that said, MEN ONLY.

Edna's mother, now recuperated from her bout with tuberculosis, saw an article in the newspaper about her daughter, "the Flying Nurse." She sent for Edna and promised to put her through medical school (another ambition of Edna's) if she would quit flying. Edna tried, but she just couldn't stay away from flying. Knowing she wouldn't be happy unless she was flying fulltime, Edna lost her mother's financial support and resigned from the navy in 1935. Years later, her mother enjoyed taking flights with her daughter and even served as copilot for about five races while in her 80s.

Edna approached commercial airlines, such as Chicago and Southern Air Lines and Braniff International Airways, for a job as a pilot. They were hiring her students, so why not hire her when she had ten times as many hours? One airline refused her for being too short, even though she was half an inch taller than a student of hers whom it did hire.

Finally, the man at Braniff asked, "Do you think people will get on an airplane if they see a woman as the pilot?"

"I don't know why not," she answered. "People get on my planes all the time."

"Well, I'm sure it hurt business. The interview is over."

Moving to New Orleans, Edna started a flight school, Air College Inc., and taught students how to fly for the airlines. When World War II arrived, she sold her school to the US Navy and went to Fort Worth, Texas, to get instrument ratings. At the end of her career, she had eight pilot ratings. She volunteered to fly for her country. Not surprisingly, she was turned down. However, the government did ask her to train male fighter pilots at Meacham Field in Texas. Her knowledge of aerobatics came in handy, because military pilots needed to know how to evade the enemy with tricky maneuvers.

When military pilot training was discontinued in February 1944, Edna fell back on her nursing skills and left the United States to work in an army hospital in the Philippines. Again, she looked for any opportunity to fly. She was recognized for flying injured soldiers out in B-25s.

After the war, Edna started another flight school, Aero Enterprises, in Fort Worth. It began as a flight training school for veterans coming back from the war. One of the flight instructors she hired was George Whyte. They fell in love and married when Edna was 43. When not teaching, she continued to enter the occasional contest. She won the Women's International Air Race in 1953. The Whytes continued to run Aero Enterprises but often talked about building their own airport.

George died before they could fulfill that dream, but Edna persevered and opened Aero Valley Airport in Roanoke, Texas. Still active in flying and teaching well into her 80s, she taught nearly 5,000 students in her lifetime, including her daughter. At the age of 83, she said, "When I grew older, I knew I could go to an old peoples' home, but I wanted one with a runway at the door. I already have that. Why should I move?"

When she died in 1992 at the age of 89, Edna had more than 35,000 flight hours, 127 air race trophies, and recognition by many groups, including the Texas Women's Hall of Fame. She also received the Charles Lindbergh Lifetime Achievement Award and was the first woman to be elected an honorary member of the Order of Daedalians, an organization of military pilots.

LEARN MORE

American Women and Flight Since 1940 by Deborah G. Douglas, Amy E. Foster, Alan D. Meyer, and Lucy B. Young (University Press of Kentucky, 2004)

"Edna Gardner Whyte" on International Women's Air and Space Museum website, http://iwasm.org/wp-blog /museum-collections/women-in-air-space-history/edna -gardner-whyte/

Rising Above It: An Autobiography—The Story of a Pioneering Woman Aviator by Edna Gardner Whyte with Ann L. Cooper (Orion Books, 1991)

≡ KATHERINE CHEUNG ≡

The First Licensed
Asian American Woman Pilot

IN 1932, A SPIRITED YOUNG woman with a big smile on her face stood next to an airplane, her hand on the propeller. Joy radiated from her face. The 27-year-old woman was a pilot. Although female pilots were still rare in 1932, she wasn't the only one, nor was she the youngest. This woman had soloed after 12.5 hours of flying lessons. Although that achievement is remarkable, she didn't hold a record for that either. What made Katherine Sui Fun Cheung extraordinary was that she was the first licensed female Asian American aviator. She raced, performed aerial acrobatics, and participated in air shows.

———•———

Born in Canton, China, in 1904, Katherine Cheung moved to the United States at age 17 to study music, first at the Los Angeles Conservatory of Music and later at California State Polytechnic University, Pomona, and the University of Southern California.

One day, she accompanied her father to Dycer Airport for a driving lesson. But instead of driving, Katherine was mesmerized by the airplanes taking off and landing. She never forgot the sight of those planes.

Years later, when she was a wife and mother, a cousin who happened to be a pilot took her up in his airplane. The experience was unlike anything she had ever experienced. She immediately signed up for flying lessons with the Chinese Aeronautical Association for five dollars.

Katherine earned her license in 1932 and became one of about 200 licensed women pilots in the United States. Of that group, she was the only one who was Asian. In her homeland of China, women weren't allowed to take lessons. She began entering air shows and competitive air events, including the Chatterton Air Race. Katherine particularly enjoyed stunt flying. The snap rolls, inverted flying, and spiral diving thrilled audiences at California county fairs.

The Chinese American community was so proud of Katherine that, with the help of famous Chinese actress Anna May Wong, they raised $2,000 to buy her a 125-horsepower Fleet biplane. In an air race from Glendale to San Diego, she came in fourth.

Three years later, in 1935, she earned her international license to fly as a commercial pilot. She was a good pilot who could handle herself in the air. One time, when she was flying back from an aviation competition in Cleveland, her compass broke, but she was still able to find her way home.

Hazel Ying Lee

Hazel Ying Lee was another early Chinese American aviator. Born in Portland, Oregon, Hazel took her first flight at the age of 19 in 1932. She joined her city's Chinese Flying Club to take lessons and earned her pilot's license the same year. Like Katherine, Hazel also heard about Japan attacking China and decided to volunteer for the Chinese Air Force—but she was rejected. She flew a commercial plane in China for a while, before returning to the United States in 1938. She joined the Women's Airforce Service Pilots (WASPs). While in training at Avenger Field in Sweetwater, Texas, she had to make an emergency landing in a farmer's field. The farmer believed she was Japanese and held her with his pitchfork until authorities could verify her identity. As a WASP, Hazel ferried pursuit or fighter aircraft from the factories to military airfields. It was while doing her job that she and another plane crashed. Her injuries were so severe that she died within a few days.

Katherine became a US citizen in 1936. She was also invited to join the Ninety-Nines. She competed against and became friends with Amelia Earhart.

China first saw airplanes in the sky around 1911, but they were almost always piloted by foreigners. The Chinese people who did have some familiarity with planes had often spent time in the United States, particularly the San Francisco area. Airplanes had to be imported from other countries, as China did not have any airplane-manufacturing facilities. By 1915, China had started its own air force, but it still needed airplanes and pilots.

The first woman pilot in China was actually Korean-born Kwon Ki-ok. After being jailed for her involvement in demonstrations in her home country, she left for China in 1920. She attended the Air Force Academy in Chongqing and was the only woman in her class. It may have been that the Chinese government wanted to put her against the Korean-born Japanese aviator Park Kyung-won. The two women met in battle only once, in 1938, and Kwon was victorious. She was put to work as a flight instructor at the Air Force Academy until she returned to Korea as a hero.

When Japan invaded China during World War II, Katherine wanted to return to China and teach volunteers to fly. She wanted to teach women as well as men. Katherine visited Chinese American communities to discuss her plans and raised more than $7,000 for a Ryan ST-A plane that she would use to train volunteer pilots.

Before Katherine Cheung could reach her goal, tragedy struck. One day, her cousin jumped in the Ryan plane and took off as a prank. However, the plane crashed, killing him. Her father, now very ill, worried about his headstrong daughter and made her promise not to fly anymore.

Katherine's promise lasted until his death. She returned to flying briefly, but it wasn't the same. Losing her friend Amelia Earhart, her cousin, and her father was just too much. Flying had lost its allure. At the age of 38, she quit flying for good and lived most of the rest of her life in Chinatown in San Francisco.

The China's Air Force Aviation Museum calls Katherine "China's Amelia Earhart." She has also been recognized by the Smithsonian National Air and Space Museum. When she was inducted into the Aviation Hall of Fame, a Chinese cultural day with a traditional Chinese lion dance was held in her honor. Katherine lived until the age of 98, dying in 2003.

Today, AirAsia has 17 female pilots. Although this number doesn't seem like much, it's a beginning in a profession and location that has long been dominated by males.

LEARN MORE

"Katherine Cheung" on Women in Aviation International website, www.wai.org/pioneers/2000pioneers.cfm

"Katherine Cheung: First Asian American Female Aviator" on Famous Chinese website, www.famouschinese.com/people/Katherine_Cheung

⫸ BERYL MARKHAM ⫷

African Bush Pilot
Crosses Atlantic

A BUZZING SOUND NEAR a village in the African bush grew louder and louder. People looked up to see an airplane. The children jumped up and cheered. The plane came closer, dropping altitude, apparently looking for a place to land. It aimed for a clearing. It looked like a tight fit, but the plane landed effortlessly and taxied for a short distance. The engine stopped, and the propeller slowly wound down. The pilot leapt out of the cockpit and onto the wing, dropping a couple of bags to the ground. A box containing medical supplies was handed to waiting hands more gently. Then the pilot jumped to the ground.

The goggles came off, followed by the helmet. Wavy brown hair tumbled out, which stopped before reaching the shoulders. The pilot was a woman; her name was Beryl Markham. As

Africa's first bush pilot, she delivered mail, supplies, and passengers wherever they were needed—even to the most remote areas.

———•———

Born in Leicester, England, in 1902, Beryl Clutterbuck moved to British-controlled Kenya with her parents when she was three years old. They weren't the only British citizens to make the move. East Africa's soil and climate made it ideal for growing crops such as coffee. Charles Clutterbuck wasn't especially talented at farming; however, he did have some success with racehorses. The British colonists enjoyed horse racing, just as they had in England. So Markham bred and trained horses for the Nairobi racetracks and taught his daughter to do the same.

Beryl's mother decided that life in Africa wasn't for her and returned to England. Beryl stayed with her father, playing with the children of the families he hired. Her father provided little supervision, allowing her to grow up fearless, which involved her being attacked by a pet lion or killing deadly mamba snakes. She learned to speak various African languages and hunt wild game with a spear. She also rode horses very well and soon became more accomplished than her father in working with horses.

Although naturally smart and a quick learner, Beryl hated being stuck in a schoolroom. She spent only two and a half years in formal schooling, learning everything else by doing or reading about it. As a teenager, she enjoyed plane rides with her friend, Denys Finch Hatton.

When her father's business failed, he returned to England. Beryl remained in Kenya and used her talent with horses to become a trainer of thoroughbreds. When she was 24, one of her horses won Kenya's greatest prize in horseracing.

Beryl met a wealthy Englishman named Mansfield Markham, whom she married in 1927. They moved to England briefly, but when the marriage ended, Beryl moved back to Kenya. Beryl couldn't stop thinking about airplanes, though. She contacted Tom Campbell Black for instruction in April 1930. After eight hours of lessons, she took to the sky by herself. A month later, she earned her pilot's license. She flew often and learned everything she could about becoming a pilot.

Her single-engine, 120-horsepower Avro Avian IV airplane had occasional engine problems, but she still decided to fly it to England less than a year after receiving her license. This flight would have been dangerous even in a good airplane, and Beryl's plane had no radio or compass.

After taking off from Nairobi, her first destination was Juba, a town in the Sudan. But a storm and engine problems prevented her from reaching the airport. Day two got her to Malakal on the Nile River. On day three, she was forced to land in the desert and make repairs to the engine herself. Problems continued, including a forced landing in a dust storm outside of Cairo.

After arranging for the British Royal Air Force to repair her plane's engine, Beryl was able to make it across the Mediterranean Sea. She wore an inner tube around her neck in case her plane went into the water. She traveled through Europe and finally reached London 23 days later.

In September 1933, Beryl became the first person in Kenya to receive a "B" license, which allowed her to hire herself out as a commercial pilot. She started as an air scout for safaris and was soon delivering supplies and mail to gold miners. She also flew sick people to hospitals and provided an air-taxi service.

Beryl heard that big prizes and fame came with setting aviation records and winning races. Although there were races in Africa, the United States and Western Europe seemed to have bigger races and bigger prizes. Beryl returned to Great Britain to decide on her next move.

Beryl wasn't the only British woman aviator. During the golden age of aviation, two of the greatest female aviators were British—Lady Mary Heath and Amy Johnson. The world first heard about Lady Mary Heath when she became the first woman to fly from Cape Town in South Africa to London in 1928. It was one of many aviation adventures and records Lady Mary would pursue. Later that year, she worked as a commercial pilot for Royal Dutch Airlines. But she loved competition the most. She was forced to leave aviation after suffering severe injuries from a crash.

Lady Heath's chief competitor was her countrywoman Amy Johnson. Dubbed "the British Amelia Earhart" by the media, she was best known as the first woman to fly solo from England to Australia. She made this journey in 1930, a year after earning her pilot's license. During World War II, Amy transported planes as part of the Air Transport Auxiliary. When a twin-engine aircraft she was flying began to have problems, she bailed out and drowned.

Although Charles Lindbergh, Amelia Earhart, and others had crossed the Atlantic, they had all been going from west to east with help from the jet stream that travels in the same direction. So far, no one had been successful flying from east to west. Beryl decided she would be the first to fly nonstop from London to New York.

Beryl borrowed a single-engine, 200-horsepower Percival Vega Gull that could reach a top speed of 163 miles per hour (262 kilometers per hour). Extra gas tanks were added so that she wouldn't have to stop during the approximately 3,500 miles (5,600 kilometers) between the cities. She took off from Abingdon, England, at 8:00 PM on September 4, 1936, against a strong headwind and stormy weather. After landing, she told the *Daily Express* newspaper, "It was a great adventure. But I'm so glad it's over. I really had a terrible time. . . . I knew I was in for it half an hour after I left. I pulled out my chart of the Atlantic and a gust of wind blew it out of my hand. I saw it floating away down to earth. . . . I had a rather bad time after that. There was a 30 mile headwind, a helluva lot of low cloud and driving rain."

Beryl had no radio on the plane. At different points, people reported spotting her—that is, until she reached the easternmost point of North America, Newfoundland. Then, she just seemed to disappear.

At that point in the journey, the fuel line to one of her gas tanks froze. This incident caused the engine to fail and the plane to rapidly lose altitude. Just before her plane went down, her fuel line warmed up, and she was able to pull up and avoid crashing into the Atlantic. When she regained her altitude, though, the fuel line froze again, this time causing her to crash into a peat bog in Nova Scotia. She climbed out of the plane, its nose buried in the muck, and greeted two nearby fishermen: "I'm Mrs. Markham. I've just flown from England."

Approximately 22 hours after her takeoff, a US Coast Guard plane came after her, and she was allowed to copilot it to New York City. She was famous on both sides of the Atlantic. She talked about entering other races but was devastated when her flight instructor and friend, Tom Campbell Black, was killed during an air race to South Africa. It made her lose any desire to fly.

There was talk of making a movie about Beryl's famous flight. That didn't happen, but Beryl, most likely with help from her third husband, Raoul Schumacher, published *West with the Night.*

Although fictionalized in parts, the book was an immediate bestseller. The autobiography covers more than her historic flight; it also touches on her life in Africa. In 2005, one of the book's true stories—about Beryl's encounter with what she believed was a tame lion—was adapted as a children's book, *The Good Lion.*

In 1952, Beryl returned to Kenya and her first love of raising and training horses. She died from pneumonia in 1986 at the age of 84.

LEARN MORE

Straight on Till Morning: The Life of Beryl Markham by Mary S. Lovell (W. W. Norton & Company, 2011)

West with the Night by Beryl Markham (North Point Press, 1982)

≣ WILLA BROWN ≣

Integrating the US Armed Forces

THE NEWSROOM OF THE *Chicago Defender* was a noisy place in 1936—filled with the sounds of clacking typewriter keys, ringing telephones, and talking reporters. But all that came to a standstill when a beautiful young woman walked in one day. She looked like a model. Wearing white breeches that disappeared into her boots, she seemed ready to ride a horse.

The city editor hurried over to her and showed her to his office. He offered her a seat, trying to ignore the eyes of his staff, who were watching them instead of doing their work.

"I'm Willa Brown. I'm an aviatrix," she announced. Early women pilots used the gender-specific word "aviatrix" rather than "aviator." "We're putting on an air show—all black pilots— at the Harlem Airport [near Chicago]. We're hoping that we can count on you, the main newspaper for our black community, to support us in publicizing our event."

The city editor, Enoch Waters, knew of one other female African American pilot. Bessie Coleman had often been reported on by the *Chicago Defender* during her lifetime. The only other African American pilots known of in Chicago were Hubert Fauntleroy Julian, also known as "the Black Eagle," and John Robinson, who was in Ethiopia at the time.

Waters would later write an article about the confidence and determination of his visitor in an article titled, WILLA BROWN VISITS THE CHICAGO DEFENDER. She told him that there were about 30 African American aviators, although most were students. Cornelius Coffey was the leader. He held a commercial pilot's license and certified mechanic's license and was a certified flight instructor. Willa neglected to add that she was married to Coffey and helped run the school.

Waters was fascinated and, with a photographer along, attended the air show, which had drawn an audience of 200 to 300. Willa was delighted he was covering the air show and offered to take the city editor up for a ride. He wrote, "She was piloting a Piper Cub, which seemed to me, accustomed as I was to commercial planes, to be a rather frail craft. It was a thrilling experience, and the maneuvers—figure eights, flip-overs and stalls—were exhilarating, though briefly frightening. I wasn't convinced of her competence until we landed smoothly."

———•———

Willa Beatrice Brown was born in Glasgow, Kentucky, on January 22, 1906, but later moved to Terre Haute, Indiana, to attend high school and college. At 21, she began teaching business in a high school in Gary, Indiana. She was the youngest high school teacher in the school system. But, dissatisfied with her life, she eventually moved to Chicago to work as a social worker. She also attended Northwestern University, where she earned her master's degree in business administration.

In the 1930s, Willa joined the Challenger Air Pilots Association, an aviation group created by Cornelius Coffey and John Robinson in Chicago. They had to teach themselves to fly because no one else would, due to their race. They also built the first airport for African Americans in Chicago. Harlem Field was located on the southwest side of Chicago. The city's airports, like its neighborhoods, were segregated at the time. Cornelius was not only a pilot and certified flight instructor, but he was also one of the best aviation mechanics in the Chicago area.

Willa took flying lessons from Cornelius and received her own private pilot's license in 1938. A year later, she had her commercial license, making her the first African American woman to hold both regular and commercial licenses. After marrying, Cornelius and Willa started the Coffey School of Aeronautics. Willa taught flight and ground school and also held a Master Mechanic Certificate.

Willa wasn't the only female African American pilot in the 1930s. There was also Janet Harmon Bragg. Like Edna Gardner Whyte, Janet was a nurse who loved to fly. With her income from working as a nurse, she bought an airplane for the Challenger Aero Club, of which she was the first president.

Janet was the first African American woman to earn a full commercial pilot's license, but it was a struggle. On her first flight test, the examiner indicated that she gave a perfect flight, but he wouldn't give her a commercial license because of her race and gender. Although she eventually received her commercial license, she couldn't get a job as a pilot. Janet volunteered to assist during World War II, both as a pilot and a nurse, but she was refused for both because of her race. She was also turned down by the Women's Airforce Service Pilots (WASPs).

Willa continued to face discrimination both as an African American and as a woman. People from her own neighborhood thought her flying was shameful because she was a woman. Willa could do nothing but shrug her shoulders and go on. But both Janet and Willa also served as role models for other African American women interested in flying.

In 1939, Willa was instrumental in forming the National Negro Airmen Association of America. The purpose of the organization was to promote African Americans as aviation cadets for the US military. So far, the government had refused admitting African Americans into programs such as the Civilian Pilot Training Program (CPTP), created in 1938 to train pilots in case the United States became involved in the war in Europe and the Pacific. As director of the Coffey School of Aeronautics, Willa pushed for black pilots to be included in programs like the CPTP. The military eventually chose the Coffey School as one of six African American schools to be part of the CPTP. Willa soon became the CPTP coordinator for Chicago.

Not long after, Willa and Cornelius began specializing in training pilots and mechanics for wartime and after the war. They taught many of the famous Tuskegee Airmen at their school and at the Air Corps pilot-training program at the Tuskegee Institute. Dorothy Layne McIntyre was one African American who received a pilot's license through the Civilian Pilot Training Program at her college in West Virginia, where she studied bookkeeping. During World War II, Dorothy taught aviation mechanics.

Willa was appointed a lieutenant in the Civil Air Patrol in 1941. She was the first African American woman to serve as an officer. She and her husband developed CAP Squadron 613 through the school. She also coordinated war-training service for the Civil Aeronautics Authority (CAA). Her efforts led to the integration of African Americans into the military. She taught aviation at both the Coffey School and at Chicago-area high schools.

Willa's idol was Bessie Coleman, so she organized an annual memorial flyover above Bessie's grave, a tradition that continued for many years.

After being instrumental in desegregating the US military in 1948, Willa returned to teaching high school. In 1972, she was appointed to the Women's Advisory Board of the Federal Aviation Administration. Her last flight was at age 86; she died of a stroke three years later.

Women like Willa and Janet Bragg worked on changing attitudes about African American pilots. Their efforts helped African Americans of both genders in aviation, and their legacies live on. Eleanor Williams became the first certified air-traffic-control specialist in 1971. Betty Payne joined the air force after college. When she heard they were planning to admit women for pilot and navigation training, she signed up for the first class and received her navigator's wings on October 12, 1977. Patrice Clarke-Washington became the first African American woman to become a captain for a commercial airline (UPS) in 1994.

LEARN MORE

"Civilian Pilot Training Program" on National Museum of the US Air Force website, www.nationalmuseum.af.mil /factsheets/factsheet.asp?id=8475

"Willa Brown" on Women Fly Resource Center website, http://womenaviators.org/WillaBrown.html

"Willa Brown Chappell" on Aviation Museum of Kentucky website, www.ket.org/trips/aviation/chappell.htm

PART III

Wartime and Military Flying

Airplanes were first used for combat during World War I. Although there were capable women pilots in the United States, none was allowed to participate in military flying. In Europe, however, female pilots from Russia and France did fly during wartime.

The world's first female combat pilot, Princess Eugenie M. Shakhovskaya of Russia, flew reconnaissance missions for the Russian tsar in 1914. This cousin of Tsar Nicholas II had received her aviator's license in 1912. Princess Eugenie was granted the rank of ensign in Russia's first aerial squad—and executed maneuvers against the Germans.

By the time World War II had started, even more qualified women pilots were available, but the United States and Western European countries refused to allow women to fly in combat. Pilots such as Nancy Love and Jackie Cochran knew the capabilities of women pilots. At the very least, they felt they should be able to free up the male pilots for combat flying.

In 1939, Germany invaded Poland. Great Britain and France declared war on Germany. While civil flying opportunities were curtailed by the war, there remained a need for pilots to deliver mail and dispatches and transport people during wartime. The greatest need was in ferrying military planes to the squadrons of the Royal Air Force. The demand was so great that it was suggested that women pilots assume ferrying duties, but many in Great Britain found the idea ridiculous.

Commercial pilot Pauline Gower was determined to bring the idea to reality, however. On January 1, 1940, Pauline was allowed to put a group of eight women pilots to work by ferrying small trainers called Tiger Moths. And thus the British Air Transport Auxiliary (ATA) was born.

As the war progressed the next year, the demand for ferrying fighter planes and bombers was greater than what the male pilots could accomplish. Ferrying duties for the women increased to cover other military aircraft. Great Britain's proximity to Germany made ferrying planes dangerous. Being shot out of the sky was a very real possibility.

Pauline was able to add more women pilots to the ATA. There were not only mixed (male and female) ferrying pools but also all-female ones. Foreign pilots were recruited by the ATA too. American pilots were the largest group of foreign members of the ATA, including a group of 25 women brought by American pilot Jacqueline Cochran. One of the pilots that Cochran recruited was her friend, Helen Richey, the first woman to train army pilots and fly a commercial airliner. The ATA, composed of 166 women and 1,152 men, delivered more than 300,000 aircraft during the war.

Although the United States hadn't declared its intentions in the war yet, it did start the Civilian Pilot Training Program (CPTP) to provide pilot training. At its start, the CPTP allowed one woman to be trained for every ten men. Within two years, however, women were banned from the program.

The United States entered World War II when Pearl Harbor was attacked on December 7, 1941. Through the efforts of women such as Jackie Cochran and Nancy Love, women pilots could aid the war effort through flying organizations like the Women's Airforce Service Pilots (WASP).

Approximately 25,000 women signed up, although many weren't eligible. Women pilots were required to be at least 5 feet tall and between the ages of 21 and 35. A high school education was also necessary, in addition to at least 200 hours of flying time. The number of flight hours was gradually reduced, while the height requirement was increased. In the end, 1,830 candidates were accepted, and 1,074 women completed the program.

According to WASP pilot Violet "Vi" Cowden, WASPs did 80 percent of all US flying from 1943 to 1944. They flew more than 60 million miles (96 million kilometers) in every type of military plane. Besides delivering aircraft to military airfields,

WASPs. *Courtesy of the US Air Force*

other duties included towing targets, flight instruction, and test-ing planes. It was a seven-day-a-week job.

Thirty-eight WASPs died in service, beginning with Corne-lia Fort, who died on March 21, 1943. She was on a ferrying flight when a male pilot clipped the wings of the plane she was flying. Fort was the first woman pilot to die in the line of duty for the US military. Gertrude Tompkins Silver disappeared while on a mission flying a P-51 to California. After an extensive search, the army ruled that she was missing and presumed dead.

Acts of sabotage against the WASPs were common on some airfields, particularly Camp Davis in North Carolina. WASPs found sugar in their planes' gas tanks (which clogs the engines); their tires blew out, radios stopped working, and planes quit in mid-air. When Lorraine Rodgers had to bail from her plane, investigators found that her rudder cables had been cut. The WASPs learned to befriend the mechanics and check their own planes before takeoff.

In the beginning, few people outside the military knew about the WASP program. Then media coverage started to grow. It was often negative, like when *Time* magazine called the WASPs "unnecessary and undesirable," even though the accident rate of the WASPs was only 9 percent compared to 11 percent among male pilots. Even with the Army Air Forces recommendation to admit the WASPs as members of the military, Congress voted against it.

As the tide turned in the war, an end to the conflict seemed evident. Rumors began circulating that the WASPs would be disbanded. The rumor became fact when the WASP program was canceled on December 20, 1944. Vi Cowden later explained, "When the men came back, they wanted their jobs back. So they deactivated us." Many of the former WASPs were unable to get flying jobs after the war ended.

Some WASPs refused to give up on recognition. They had served their country, and some had died in service for their country. Thirty-three years later, Congress voted to give the WASPs veteran's status, retroactive to their initial service. In the Senate, the vote was unanimous. On November 23, 1977, President Jimmy Carter signed a bill into law:

> Officially declaring the Women Airforce Service Pilots as having served on active duty in the Armed Forces of the United States for purposes of laws administered by the Veterans Administration.

Just as surprising as how long it took for the WASPs to be recognized was the fact that that no branch of the military accepted female pilots until 1974 or later. The first to do so was the navy, which admitted six women to the US Naval Flight Training School. The first to graduate was Commander Barbara Allen Rainey.

The navy's first combat pilot was Lieutenant Kara Spears Hultgreen. She was killed in 1994, when the left engine of her F-14 stalled during an attempt to land on the USS *Abraham Lincoln* about 50 miles (80 kilometers) off the coast of San Diego.

Later in 1974, the army began training female helicopter pilots. The first woman army pilot was Second Lieutenant Sally D. Woolfolk, who primarily flew UH-1 Huey helicopters.

Women were admitted to the Air Force pilot training program in 1976, navigator training in 1977, and fighter-pilot training in 1993, the same year that American women were first allowed to fly in combat. The 1976 program graduated 10 women, including Captain Connie Engle, who went on to become the first woman to fly the T-41 Mescalero and T-37 Tweet aircrafts solo. She was also the first woman to lead a two-ship formation.

Both the Air National Guard and the Coast Guard had their first female pilots in the late 1970s. It took the Marine Corps a little longer; Major Sarah M. Deal became the first female Marine Corps pilot in April 1995.

According to the Department of Defense in 2011, the air force has the greatest percentage of women on active military duty: 19.1 percent. In 2005, for the first time in the history of the Air Force, a woman was allowed to join the legendary high-performance jet team, the Thunderbirds. Two years later, for the first time in naval history, a woman commanded a fighter squadron. All branches of the US military restricted women military aviators until January 2013. At that time, Secretary of Defense Leon Panetta issued a directive lifting all restrictions of women in combat. All military branches must submit a plan for integrating women by May 15, 2013, and integration must be complete by the beginning of 2016.

≣ JACQUELINE COCHRAN ≣
Women Pilots Can Make a Difference

JACQUELINE "JACKIE" COCHRAN KNEW women pilots could make a difference. In 1939, she wrote to First Lady Eleanor Roosevelt suggesting that women pilots be trained in order to free male pilots for combat roles. Eleanor Roosevelt was no stranger to the skills of women pilots. She had been a friend of Amelia Earhart's, whom she had often talked to about women flying. Roosevelt recommended that Jackie talk to General Hap Arnold.

General Hap Arnold headed the US Army Air Forces, which focused on military flying and eventually became the US Air Force. He asked Jackie to study the women pilots in Great Britain. She took 25 female pilots to Great Britain to train with ATA. She also demonstrated how women could be of service when she became the first woman to ferry a bomber across the Atlantic Ocean.

While Jackie was in Great Britain, Nancy Harkness Love established the Women's Auxiliary Ferrying Squadron (WAFS) through the Ferry Command of the Army Air Forces. Nancy picked the 25 best women pilots to ferry military planes throughout the United States.

General Arnold asked Jackie to return in 1942 to begin a women's flight-training program. The Women's Flying Training Detachment (WFTD) began in November when the first 28 recruits of the WFTD arrived in Houston to begin training. At the same time, Nancy Love's WAFS pilots flew their first mission—transporting Piper Cubs from Lock Haven, Pennsylvania, to Mitchell Field in Newcastle, England.

In February 1943, the Houston WFTD School closed, and all recruits for the program were required to report to Sweetwater, Texas. West of Dallas and Abilene, Sweetwater was dry and dusty and boasted a resident population of rattlesnakes. But it was also the location of Avenger Field, a training base for the Army Air Forces.

Nancy Love.
Courtesy of the US Air Force

Six months after Avenger Field became the training base for the WFTD, the government decided to merge the two women pilot programs, Nancy's WAFS and Jackie's WFTD, into the Women Airforce Service Pilots (WASP). Jackie became the director.

At Avenger Field, the women went through exactly the same training as the male recruits had. They trained mainly with the PT-19, but they also performed basic training with the BT-17 before advancing to the AT-6.

Unlike many early and famed women aviators, Jackie never had the ambition to be a pilot. She hadn't pined to be in the air when she was a little girl—she had been too busy just trying to survive.

———•———

Born Bessie Pittman in the rural Florida panhandle, Jackie knew only her sawmill town and its cotton fields as a child. Poverty was a way of life, and sometimes she stole chickens so that her family could eat. In her autobiography, she wrote that she didn't wear shoes until she was eight years old.

She picked cotton at an early age; soon she graduated from that to sweeping floors and shampooing hair in a beauty salon. Along the way, she changed her name from Bessie Pittman to Jacqueline Cochran. By 13, she was cutting hair and developing her own list of customers. Although she tried nursing school, she was never comfortable with it.

Instead, Jackie took her beautician skills to New York City in 1929, working at the popular salon called Antoine de Paris at Saks Fifth Avenue. Invited to various social gatherings, she met important people. At one dinner in 1932, she met millionaire Floyd Odlum. To him, she confessed a dream of owning a cosmetics company. He advised her that flying was the best way to cover her territory during the economic depression.

She immediately began taking flying lessons. Within three weeks, she had her license. Jackie discovered something about flying when she was in the air: it felt right. She had a certain affinity for piloting. Later, she would say, "At that moment, when I paid for my first lesson, a beauty operator ceased to exist, and an aviator was born."

Two days after earning her license, Jackie took off for a Canadian sports pilots' gathering in Montreal. Flying that distance solo made her realize how much she still had to learn about flying, including instrument flying and reading a compass and maps. Navigating an airplane with only the use of the instruments was necessary if one planned on being a serious pilot.

Tired of East Coast weather, Jackie enrolled in the Ryan Flying School in San Diego, California, in 1933. She was embarrassed about her lack of education and had an aversion to taking written tests and sitting in classrooms. She found someone to give her one-on-one instruction, and she soaked up as much as she could.

When she finished advanced flight training, she began entering races. The first major race she entered was the MacRobertson Air Race from London to Melbourne, which carried a $75,000 prize. She planned to compete in a plane with the nickname "Gee Bee." However, the Gee Bee was a difficult and often dangerous plane to fly. Problems with the plane's flaps and mislabeled gas tank switches forced her to touch down in Romania. She was also forced to drop out of the 1935 Bendix cross-country race because of mechanical problems.

Jackie believed in hard work. While she was learning to fly, she was also launching her cosmetics company, Jacqueline Cochran Cosmetics. Her determination paid off. By 1935, she was not only an accomplished pilot but also the owner of a successful cosmetics company. Another high point came in 1936, when she married Floyd Odlum. She also began meeting other women pilots and became friends with Amelia Earhart. Like Amelia, Jackie also served as president of the Ninety-Nines at one time.

Jackie was a very competitive person. She wanted to win the races she entered, but mechanical problems prevented her from even finishing. Her luck eventually changed. In the 1937 Bendix, she came in third overall and was the first-place female finisher. The next year, she won the whole thing—coming in before any other pilot, male or female.

In the 1938 Bendix race, she piloted a silver Seversky P-35 fighter plane, attempting to fly the 2,042 miles (3,286 kilometers) from Los Angeles to Cleveland. As she approached her destination, she had only enough gasoline in her tanks for a few minutes, but it was enough. At 2:23 PM, she crossed the finish line, winning the Bendix in 8 hours, 10 minutes, and 31 seconds. Due to her plane having a new fuel system, she was the first pilot to complete the race nonstop. She was also honored with the General William Mitchell Memorial Award, given for outstanding contribution to aviation.

Not only did Jackie begin winning races, but she began setting records as well. Many were speed records, but she also broke a woman's altitude record, reaching 33,000 feet (10,000 meters) in 1937. She continued to break records until war broke out in Europe.

As soon as the Women Airforce Service Pilots program was fully operational, Jackie's graduates didn't just ferry planes to airfields. They also trained B-17 turret gunners and staff pilots, towed targets, and worked as test pilots.

In January 1944, the US War Department announced that WASP accident rates were actually lower than those of the male pilots. But when male pilots began returning from Europe and the Pacific, they wanted their jobs back. Although the WASPs had proven invaluable during wartime, the government ended the program.

Jackie was disappointed, although she was the first civilian woman ever recognized with the US Distinguished Service Medal. She was also the only woman from the United States to be an eyewitness to Japan's surrender in the Philippines (the US military was fairly strict about keeping women out of the war zone, but Jackie knew enough important people to be an exception to the rule); she then entered Japan after the war and was the first American woman allowed to do so. She later witnessed the Nuremberg trials in Germany.

The First Woman to Break the Sound Barrier

Jackie Cochran climbed into the cockpit of a F-86 Sabre jet one day in 1953. She completed her preflight tasks and then began taxiing down the runway for takeoff. She gloried in the feeling of being up in the sky—there was nothing else quite like it. And the speed! She pushed the throttle, feeling vibrations as she flew faster. Jackie became aware of a voice coming through her headset. "You did it! You did it!" said Chuck Yeager, an Air Force pilot and good friend of Jackie's. In 1953, he and Jackie were now a club of two. They were the only two people to have broken Mach 1, better known as the sound barrier.

When World War II ended, Jackie returned to air races and setting new records in the 1950s and 1960s. She set some of these records while she worked as a test pilot for Northrop and Lockheed. She set eight speed records in a row in a Northrop T-38. Then a few years later, she set three more speed records in a Lockheed F-104 Starfighter jet. During that time, she flew more than 1,429 miles per hour (2,300 kilometers per hour), the fastest a woman had ever flown.

In the 1970s, Jackie began having serious problems with her heart. She needed a pacemaker, which would prevent her from continuing the type of flying she was doing. She did her best to adjust to life without flying. But when her husband died in 1976, her health went downhill. She died on August 9, 1980. Services were held at the US Air Force Academy in Colorado Springs, Colorado.

Jackie Cochran won more than 200 awards for her flying. She holds more speed, altitude, and distance records than any other pilot—male or female. Jackie Cochran, a 14-time winner of the Harmon Trophy, awarded to the best female pilot of the year, made her mark on aviation.

Jackie didn't go to college; she never even finished high school. She learned by listening and asking questions. She believed that with hard work, she could accomplish anything. Perhaps, most of all, she learned to reinvent herself. She went from being a poor, uneducated, barefoot child to becoming the successful owner of a cosmetics company and then one of the best pilots the world has ever seen. Jackie Cochran's life is a true rags-to-riches story and a shining example of how anything is possible.

LEARN MORE

Fly Girls (documentary), *American Experience*, PBS (2006)

"Jacqueline Cochran" on the National Aviation Hall of Fame website, www.nationalaviation.org/cochran-jacqueline

Jackie Cochran: An Autobiography by Jacqueline Cochran and Maryann Bucknum Brinley (Bantam, 1987)

"Jackie Cochran Biography" on the National WASP World War II Museum website, http://waspmuseum.org/jackie -cochran-biography/

Jackie Cochran: Pilot in the Fastest Lane by Doris L. Rich (University Press of Florida, 2010)

≣ VIOLET COWDEN ≣
Determined WASP

"You can't fly," the doctor told her. But Violet Cowden, often known as Vi to her friends, knew he was wrong. She could and did fly any chance she got. She knew what the doctor really meant was that she didn't meet the height and weight requirements for the Women's Airforce Service Pilots. At five feet, two inches and 92 pounds, she was two inches too short and eight pounds too light.

"Give me a week," she said.

She began eating a diet of fattening food to gain weight, which was more difficult than it sounded. Right up until she got on the scale again, she was stuffing food down. Someone told her to eat several bananas and drink a lot of water before getting on the scale, so she did.

In anticipation of the doctor's verdict, Vi fluffed up her hair and tied a scarf on her head. With all her might, she stood up as straight as she could. Holding her breath, she waited.

"How did you do it?" he asked.

Vi showed him her stomach, distended with all the water she had been drinking. He laughed, but then he signed her physical examination form. She had passed.

Why was it so important to Vi to be a pilot? It's all she had ever wanted to do. Vi may have been tiny, but her courage and will to succeed were gigantic.

———•———

Violet Clara Thurn was born on October 1, 1916, in a three-room sod house on a South Dakota farm. One of her first memories was watching the hawks fly. "I want to be up in the sky with the birds," she told her family.

She attended a country school about a mile and a half from home. Her father believed in the importance of an education, so he made sure his children never missed a day. When the weather was nice, Violet and her siblings would walk. When it snowed, their father would attach a sleigh to the horses for the ride to school and heat up rocks to keep their feet warm for the journey.

The high school was farther away—four miles. During the winter months, Vi had to stay in town, working for her room and board. Once, when she was a senior in high school, a barnstormer landed his Cessna nearby. The Depression was in its midst and money was tight, but Vi's boyfriend paid five dollars for her to take a ride.

After graduating from Black Hills State University, Vi's first job was teaching first grade in Spearfish, South Dakota. One day, she and a friend went to the small airport where the friend's husband was taking flying lessons. Vi decided right then and there that she would too. She approached the teacher, Clyde Ice, and told him she wanted to learn to fly. He looked at her and grinned. "Come on. I think you'll make a damn good pilot. Let's go."

Vi earned $110 a month from her job, and her flying lessons cost her $10 a month. She didn't own a car or even know how to drive one, so she rode her bicycle six miles to the airport in the mornings for her lessons. Then she would ride her bicycle back and get ready to teach her first graders. At night, she returned to the airport for ground school. She didn't quite realize how important flying was to her until one particular day when she came to school.

"Did you go flying this morning?" one little boy asked her.

"Why, yes, I did. How did you know?" Vi asked.

"Because you always look so happy after flying."

Vi earned her pilot's license and flew single-engine planes with small motors, such as Aeroncas and Cubs. After Pearl Harbor was attacked, Vi tried to volunteer for the Civil Air Patrol but never received a reply. She had started training for a navy program, the WAVES (Women Accepted for Volunteer Emergency Service), when she got a telegram. It instructed her to report for the fourth class: Vi was one of the 1,830 accepted for the WASP program. The program had been moved to Sweetwater, Texas, and Vi was a member of Sweetwater's first class of WASPs.

Recruits had to pass 23 weeks of ground school, physical training, and military flying. They had to know subjects such as math, physics, and meteorology. And they had to pass classes in map reading, navigation, engine repair, Morse code, and military regulation. In short, the women underwent the exact same training that the men did.

Each day, Vi and the other women were up by six in the morning. One semester, she had ground school in the morning and flight training in the afternoon. The next semester, the order was reversed. Vi started her training in a 150-horsepower Fairchild PT-19. As she progressed through the training, she moved up to more powerful airplanes, such as the BT-13 Valiant and the AT-6. She practiced night flying, for the first time ever, in an AT-17 Bobcat.

One day, a male colonel overheard Vi telling a classmate that the flight training wasn't that hard. He decided to give her something to groan about and had her do five evaluated test flights in five days. Vi said that when it was over, she was a basket case.

As civil service employees, the trainees had to pay for their own clothing, food, and lodging. Vi's flight suit was a man's size 44 that she wore throughout her service. After her first solo flight on March 5, 1943, she was commissioned in the WASPs.

Vi graduated from training in August 1943. When Jackie Cochran gave her the silver wings, Vi vowed that no one would ever take them away from her. (When pilots finished training, they were awarded their wings, a pin that would go on their uniform. Cochran fought to make certain that the 1,074 women pilots who graduated from her program were awarded silver wings.)

Vi was assigned to Air Transport Command at Love Field in Dallas, Texas. She continued training in Brownsville, Texas, with four male pilots, learning to fly pursuit planes in an AT-6. In pursuit planes, pilots couldn't see ahead of them; they had to look out the sides to see where they were going. In the beginning, the instructor wouldn't let her fly. But when he made a bad landing and tried to blame it on her, she finally spoke up to defend herself. The next day, he let her fly—and had to admit that she knew was she was doing.

In World War II, WASPs flew planes to different destinations. Vi was one of 114 pursuit pilots assigned to pick up planes and deliver them to military airfields in either Newark, New Jersey, or Long Beach, California. Her favorite plane was the P-51, which was known for its speed and fuel capacity and was used to guard bombers during missions. Military historians say that the P-51 was a big part of winning World War II. Vi even delivered the Tuskegee Airmen's first P-51.

Like most of the WASPs, Vi worked every day of the week and flew in all kinds of weather and conditions. When the male pilots began coming home in late 1944, they wanted their jobs back. Vi and the others WASPs went to the airlines for jobs. They were told they were qualified, "but we can't give you the job because you're a woman."

WASPs. *Courtesy of the US Air Force*

The women pilots didn't earn as much as the male pilots, nor were they entitled to benefits because the WASPs weren't officially in the military. Vi worked hard on behalf of her fellow WASPs; she contacted members of Congress and had people sign petitions. Finally, in 1977, the WASPs' work was recognized when President Jimmy Carter granted them military status, making them eligible for all the benefits war veterans were due.

When she was 89, Vi parachuted out of an airplane. A year later, she and a veteran friend participated in a simulated dogfight over a California airport. She also went paragliding and finally felt like the hawks that she used to envy.

Vi Cowden continued flying into her 90s. During her time in the WASPs, Vi had flown eight different military planes. On May 1, 2009, she got the chance to pilot her favorite plane once more; 65 years had passed since she had last flown a P-51. She flew a P-51C Mustang from San Diego to Long Beach, California, an experience she called a dream come true. As soon as she stepped into the cockpit, she remembered how flying her first P-51 felt.

In March 2010, almost 70 years after flying for their country, Vi and the other 300 WASPs who were still living received the Congressional Gold Medal for service to the United States. The Congressional Gold Medal, the highest honor given to civilians, is given for outstanding acts of service to the United States.

A documentary, *Wings of Silver: The Vi Cowden Story*, was made about her life. She was also an active member of the Ninety-Nines and participated in a "living history" project in which World War II veterans spoke at high schools.

When Vi Cowden died at age 94, obituaries everywhere referred to her as a wartime-plane pilot. She would have enjoyed that recognition.

LEARN MORE

A WASP Among Eagles: A Woman Military Test Pilot in World War II by Ann Carl (Smithsonian Institution Press, 2010)

WASP Pilot Violet Cowden (video) on History.com, www .history.com/videos/wasp-pilot-violet-cowden#wasp -pilot-violet-cowden

≣ VALENTINA GRIZODUBOVA ≣

The Soviet Amelia Earhart

WHILE AMERICAN WOMEN WERE restricted to administrative flying missions during wartime, more than a thousand Russian women flew combat missions. Valentina Grizodubova was one of them.

Women had served in combat positions in the Soviet Union as early as World War I. Together, Russia and the surrounding countries were one country, known as the Soviet Union, from 1919 to 1991. Except for Turkey, which had one female military pilot in Sabiha Gokcen, the Soviet Union was the only country with women who flew in combat.

Valentina made more than 200 military flights during World War II, including bombing missions against Germany. She was promoted to colonel and served as commander of a long-range bomber squadron of 300 men.

"In my experience, girls make just as good pilots as men," she said in 1942. "You cannot judge by appearance. I know girls so quiet and apparently timid that they blush when spoken to, yet they pilot bombers over Germany without qualm. No country at war today can afford to ignore the tremendous reservoir of woman power."

———•———

Sometimes referred to as the Soviet Union's Amelia Earhart, Valentina Grizodubova was born January 18, 1910 (though her birth date is sometimes listed as January 31 because her country changed to a different type of calendar after her birth). By the time Valentina reached adulthood, the Soviet Union had embraced aviation. Most women received flight training through the Society for Cooperation in Defense and Aviation-Chemical Development (OSOAVIAKhIM). By 1941, between one-fourth and one-third of all Soviet pilots were female.

Before the war, Valentina taught flying. She also tested how far she could push the altitude, speed, and distance of an airplane. Records weren't being set only in the United States. Valentina set six world records, including a women's long-distance nonstop flight record, which she later broke. On October 28, 1937, Valentina, together with Marina Raskova, flew an AIR-12 and established a new long-distance nonstop flight record for women.

Less than a year later, the two women, along with Paulina Ossipenko as copilot, set a women's distance record when they flew from Moscow to Vladivostok in the Far East—a distance of 4,000 miles (6,450 kilometers). They covered it in 26 hours and 29 minutes. The trio flew an ANT-37, which was a converted long-range DB-2 bomber. Valentina named the plane *Rodina*, which means "motherland."

During the flight, the group relied primarily on radio signals to navigate, as the overcast skies made physical landmarks almost impossible to find. As they flew farther from civilization, they stopped receiving radio signals. They flew until they ran out of fuel and had to make a forced landing in a swamp.

For three days, no one knew what had happened to the women. Stuck in the wilderness in the rain, they chased off wild animals, including bears and even a lynx that decided to explore their cockpit. Valentina, Marina, and Paulina were finally located in marshy land near the Siberian-Manchoukuo border. They were returned to Moscow and celebrated as heroes and

Bridge of Wings

Many years later, a group of women thought it was time to re-create the flight that made Valentina Grizodubova, Marina Raskova, and Paulina Ossipenko famous. American pilots Nikki Mitchell and Rhonda Miles, both from Nashville, flew around the world in 49 days in 1998. When they landed in Moscow, they joined two Russian female pilots, Khalide Makagonova and Natalia Vinokourova, to re-create the 1938 trip across Russia to the southeastern tip of Siberia. They called their commemorative flight the Bridge of Wings tour.

The American women landed in Moscow on July 23, 1998. The next day, they met with approximately 50 survivors of the Soviet Night Witches and other groups of World War II women pilots. Four days later, the four women began their journey. Sixty years had passed since the original respected aviators; they were even awarded the Order of Lenin, one of their country's highest honors.

World War II was already a major conflict in Europe before the United States joined. In the Great Patriotic War (what Russians called World War II), the Soviet Union suffered such a large number of casualties in 1941 that the government ordered all women without children to join in battling Nazi Germany.

Marina Raskova, who flew with Valentina on the historic flight of 1938, asked Soviet leader Joseph Stalin to form female military-pilot squadrons. She had been teaching military navigation to Soviet men for a few years and then received her pilot's

flight, so the women had modern tools to make the flight to the town of Osipenko a little safer. Still, the flight involved passing over glaciers and large, isolated areas of swamp. Russia is the largest country in the world, but much of it is uninhabitable. Yet at every stop, the pilots were greeted with enthusiasm. In Kazan, Russia, their first stop after Moscow, a brass band waited. As the women deplaned, they were serenaded with 1940s American big band music, including "Chattanooga Choo Choo." In even the smallest villages, Russians turned out to greet them. In Olyokminsk, the mayor and groups of dancers were waiting.

When they reached their destination of Osipenko, the women of the Bridge of Wings tour dropped flowers where the *Rodina* had been forced to land. The townspeople took the women from their hotel to a monument of Russia's most famous women pilots. Everywhere they looked, they saw tributes to the pilots of the *Rodina*.

license in 1935. In October 1941, the all-female 122nd Composite Air Group was formed to train pilots and navigators for new regiments.

Marina chose women with a minimum of 500 flying hours to serve as fighter or bomber pilots. She oversaw all the training, which was intensive, with ten courses and two hours of drills daily. Most, like Raisa Surnachevskaya, were young, in their late teens or early 20s. Raisa was 21 and four months pregnant when she shot down two German planes.

Lilya Litvyak, also 21, was another Soviet pilot. Although she was so small that the pedals of her plane had to be adjusted so she could reach them, Lilya (or Lily) became a senior lieutenant and served in three fighter regiments. She painted a white lily on her airplane that some enemy pilots mistook for a rose. Lilya became known as the White Rose of Stalingrad; she also became the first woman in the world to shoot down an enemy aircraft on September 13, 1942, when she shot down two German fighters over Stalingrad. In all, she shot down 12 German planes. However Lilya was shot down less than a year later; she was one of nine Soviet aircraft facing off against 40 enemy planes.

Many Russian women flew with male regiments, but three of the regiments from the 122nd started out as all female—the 586th Fighter Aviation Regiment, the 588th Night Bomber Aviation Regiment, and the 587th Day Bomber Aviation Regiment commanded by Major Marina Raskova. The 588th Regiment, later renamed the 46th, flew 24,000 combat missions. They were so successful in their nighttime bombing missions that the Germans began calling them "the Night Witches." The Russian female pilots found it amusing when they surprised German pilots, who weren't expecting to hear female voices in the skies.

When World War II ended, 23 women received Hero of the Soviet Union medals, but Marina wasn't there to receive hers.

A Shared War Experience

Although the WASPs and the Soviet pilots fought for the same side during World War II, they believed they were worlds apart. After all, what could they have in common? Plenty, they found out. The WASPs arrived in Moscow in 1990 for what Violet Cowden described as a wonderful experience. They met 120 female World War II pilots. In 2002, the WASPs returned, although both groups were smaller.

American and Soviet women pilots were discarded at the end of the war, and for many years, their contributions were ignored. Both groups had to wear military uniforms, which meant donning men's uniforms that were many sizes too large. Russian pilots said that military leaders even gave them men's underwear. They had shared dangerous assignments, but most of all they shared a strong sense of patriotism. Fighting for their country was worth it all.

The plane she was flying had been caught in a heavy snowstorm on January 4, 1943, while transferring her regiment to the front. The plane crashed, killing all on board, including Marina. Her funeral was the war's first state funeral. Her ashes were entombed in the Kremlin Wall as a sign of respect.

Valentina became the most decorated woman of the Soviet Union, receiving the Hero of the Soviet Union medal in addition to the Order of the Red Star, the Order of the Red Banner, and the medal of a member of the Supreme Soviet.

After retiring from the military in 1946, Valentina worked in civil aviation, one of only a few women who were able to continue in aviation. Even with everything the many Soviet pilots had accomplished, as soon as the war was over, they were strongly encouraged to return home and serve as wives and mothers. Valentina spent the remainder of her life living quietly with her family, including her husband, an army pilot captain, and her son. She died in 1993 at the age of 83.

LEARN MORE

Flying for Her Country: The American and Soviet Women Military Pilots of World War II by Amy Goodpaster Strebe (Potomac Books, 2009)

Night Witches: The Amazing Story of Russia's Women Pilots in World War II by Bruce Myles (Academy Chicago Publishers, 1990)

Women in War and Resistance: Selected Biographies of Soviet Women Soldiers by Kazimiera J. Cottam (Focus Publishing, 1998)

Women Military Pilots of World War II: A History with Biographies of American, British, Russian and German Aviators by Lois K. Merry (McFarland, 2010)

≣ HANNA REITSCH ≣

The World's First Female Test Pilot

THE LAST DAYS OF World War II were exciting and dangerous—exciting for the United States, Great Britain, the Soviet Union, and other countries (known collectively as the Allies) because they were about to win the war. But Berlin, the center of power for Nazi Germany, was burning. Russian tanks had entered the city and were firing at anyone who didn't immediately surrender. Streets were destroyed, full of huge holes from the shells. One of those shots hit a small airplane. Somehow, though, the plane was still able to land in the center of the destruction. It was the only German plane that had been able to get to Berlin during the last days of the war. The pilot, Hanna Reitsch, had orders to bring General Robert Ritter von Greim to the German leader, Adolf Hitler.

The shot that hit Hanna's plane caused an injury to one of von Greim's feet. Hanna had to help him to Hitler's underground bunker. After two days in the bunker, Hanna took off; heavy gunfire showered her plane.

Unlike in the Soviet Union, female military pilots weren't allowed in Germany in World War II, with one exception: Hanna Reitsch. Fascism, the political beliefs adopted by Germany and Italy in the early 20th century, restricted women to the roles of wife and mother. Working outside the home was frowned upon. Despite this, some did have jobs, but very few were pilots. (Another German woman, Melitta Schiller, received the Iron Cross for performing about 1,500 test dives of German dive-bombers. But Hanna was Germany's top female aviator and a favorite of Hitler's.)

As the world's first female test pilot, Hanna tested many Nazi planes and weapons, even rocket-powered planes that would later lead to space travel. But her daring landing and takeoff in the last days of the Third Reich are what most people remember about her. She was one of the last people to see Adolf Hitler alive.

———•———

Hanna was born on March 29, 1912, in the eastern German province of Hirschberg, Silesia (now known as Jelenia Góra, Poland). Hanna's ophthalmologist father wanted her to be a doctor. She wanted to fly. She planned to combine the two and become a flying missionary doctor.

Hanna recalled jumping off a balcony when she was four, trying to fly like a bird. In her 1955 autobiography, *The Sky My Kingdom*, she wrote, "The longing grew in me, grew with every bird I saw go flying across the azure summer sky, with every cloud that sailed past me on the wind, till it turned to a deep, insistent homesickness, a yearning that went with me everywhere and could never be stilled."

She grew up during World War I and the immediate years afterward. The Versailles Treaty from World War I barred Germany from building "war planes." Because of this restriction, gliders (which were like planes but had no engines) became popular in Germany.

At age 20, while in medical school, Hanna began taking glider lessons. She became an excellent glider pilot and was the first woman to fly over the Alps in a glider. She left medical school and began teaching and taking on stunt-pilot work in the movies. She even participated in an expedition to study South American weather.

Hanna competed all over the world. She held several glider records and became the first woman to earn the Silver Soaring

What Is a Glider?

Gliders are simply planes without engines, but they range from paper airplanes to the space shuttle. How does something fly without an engine? A regular airplane flies by the aid of four forces: thrust, lift, drag, and weight. In comparison, a glider has no thrust and therefore will eventually fall to earth because it can't generate enough lift. Gliders typically get their initial lift from a powered aircraft that pulls the glider before releasing it. However, when a glider pilot finds a pocket of air, he or she can actually gain altitude from updrafts.

Medal for a cross-country flight. She set more than 40 world records, including women's world records for glider altitude, which she earned by reaching 9,200 feet (2,800 meters); nonstop distance flight, which she earned by traveling 190 miles (305 kilometers); and nonstop gliding, which she earned by staying in the air for 11.5 hours.

Hanna flew other aircraft as they became available. In 1938, she became the first helicopter pilot and took the first indoor helicopter flight in the Deutschlandhalle, an exhibition hall in Berlin. She described this way: "Professor Focke and his technicians standing below grew ever smaller as I continued to rise straight up, 50 meters, 75 meters, 100 meters. Then I gently began to throttle back and the speed of ascent dwindled until I was hovering motionless in midair. This was intoxicating! I thought of the lark, so light and small of wing, hovering over the summer fields. Now man had wrested from him his lovely secret."

As one of the first working helicopters, the Focke-Wulf Fw 61 received a lot of attention. Hanna demonstrated it every night for two weeks and even showed famed pilot Charles Lindbergh what it could do. She set the first helicopter records for endurance, speed, and altitude. Hanna's skills attracted attention, and soon she was recruited to be a test pilot by the Luftwaffe. This German air force, which Hitler had been secretly growing, became an official branch of the Third Reich's military in 1935. After its existence became public, twenty squadrons were ready to go to war, and thousands more pilots joined up too. Hanna recommended an all-woman squadron, but that idea was rejected.

When Germany went to war, Hanna began testing various aircraft, including gliders, airplanes, helicopters, and weapons. She called German warplanes "guardians of the portals of peace." She became much in demand and was even given the honorary title of "flight captain."

Hanna tested the first operational jet fighter, the twin-engine Me-262 Schwalbe ("swallow"). She also tested one bomber that had steel blades installed on the edges of its wings. It was developed to cut heavy steel cables attached to barrage balloons. Barrage balloons were a ground-based air-defense apparatus used to keep attacking planes from getting too close or accurate with weapons.

Perhaps the most dangerous plane Hanna tested was the Fieseler Fi 103R, intended to be a manned flying bomb. In an ideal scenario, the pilot would detach from the plane after directing the bomb toward its target, but the canopy made the chance of pilot survival very small. Hanna didn't recommend the Fieseler Fi 103R, not because it was likely to be a suicide mission but because she felt like the frame was unstable. She also had concerns about the engine's uncontrollable shaking and its noise level.

Hanna was a talented pilot who supported Hitler and the Third Reich. No one knows how much she knew about the events of the Nazi regime outside of flying—but she clearly admired Hitler. As the only woman awarded both the Iron Cross and Luftwaffe Diamond Clasp, she continued to wear the Iron Cross long after the war ended, even though many regarded it as a symbol of Nazi Germany.

Hanna left Hitler's bunker as the war was ending, and two days later, she surrendered to Allied forces. She was interrogated over the next 18 months. When asked if she was a Nazi, Hanna replied, "I was a German, well known as an aviator and as one who cherished an ardent love of her country and had done her duty to the last."

When she left the bunker, she had carried with her a poison capsule filled with cyanide. Cyanide poisoning was one of the methods Hitler chose for his own death. Why didn't she take it as well? During her interrogation with the US Army, on October 9, 1945, Hanna testified that the thought of never flying again stopped her. (Years later, she showed the capsule to another glider owner, which seems to speak to her love of flying.) Also, she realized that Hitler was growing more disturbed in his last days.

After the war, Hanna returned to flying and sharing her love of flying with other women pilots. Concentrating on gliders, Hanna won the bronze medal in the International Gliding Championships in Madrid, Spain, in 1953. She went on to set two more glider altitude records.

In 1961, the former test pilot for the Nazis met president John F. Kennedy and was accepted for membership in the American Test Pilots' Association. When she was 65, she flew a glider almost 600 miles (970 kilometers) in Pennsylvania and set a new distance record for gliders. A year later, she died of a heart attack.

Whirly-Girls

Women airplane pilots were rare. Even rarer were helicopter pilots. In 1955, six of the thirteen known female helicopter pilots from the United States, France, and Germany decided to band together as a group called the Whirly-Girls. Their motto: "Their eggbeaters aren't in the kitchen." (The rotors of a helicopter were often referred to as "eggbeaters.") Today there are more than 1,000 Whirly-Girls hailing from 30 countries.

LEARN MORE

From Nazi Test Pilot to Hitler's Bunker by Dennis Piszkiewicz (Praeger, 1997)

Hanna Reitsch: Flying for the Fatherland by Judy Lomax (John Murray Publishers, 1990)

"Hanna Reitsch: The Last Interview" on YouTube, www .youtube.com/watch?v=4vxxHyl46co

PART IV

All Part of the Job

For many years, aviation didn't present many career opportunities for women. The lucky few had money or sponsors, but even sponsorships gradually dropped off as airplanes became more common. Eventually, it seemed as though everyone had seen airplanes flying overhead and had even experienced riding in airplanes. There were also more pilots, which meant fewer available jobs. And those jobs usually went to men.

For many women, this wouldn't do. They didn't have the time or money to make aviation a hobby. They enjoyed flying and using the specific skills that piloting a plane required. They wanted jobs doing what they did best: flying.

During the 1930s, commercial airlines developed as airplanes increased in size in order to take passengers. A nurse in Cresco, Iowa, believed that these passenger airlines should have someone on board whose job it was to take care of the passengers while the pilot flew. Ellen Church persuaded Boeing Air Transport to use a cabin crew. The first passenger planes to use them held only twelve passengers, and the first flight attendants were required to be single women younger than 25. They also had to help the ground crews push the airplanes into the hangers. Flight attendants, or stewardesses as they were called then, became a successful addition to the flying experience.

Although Helen Richey piloted a commercial airline around the same time, commercial airlines took longer to accept women in the cockpit. Women such as Captain Beverly Burns and Captain Lynn Rippelmeyer persisted, but it wasn't until the 1970s and 1980s that women pilots began making inroads into the commercial airline industry. Slowly, determined women entered the male-dominated profession.

Rather than trying to obtain jobs in commercial aviation, other women pilots pursued the entertainment route. What mattered most about that type of flying wasn't gender, but how well they flew. Barnstorming faded with the introduction of aviation regulations, but stunt flying and performing in aerobatic shows became just as big. After sound became a part of movies, action adventure movies began using stunt flyers. Because pilots weren't receiving decent wages, in September 1931 Pancho Barnes and other flyers formed the Associated Motion Picture Pilots to negotiate pay, insurance, and safety standards. Today's movie stunt pilots are members of the Motion Picture Pilots Association (MPPA), a union that monitors entertainment aviation.

Other women found industries where their piloting skills could be useful. Mary Barr became the US Forest Service's first woman pilot in 1974. By 1983, Charlotte Larson had become the first woman to work as a smoke jumper aircraft captain. Smoke jumpers are an important part of firefighting teams in wilderness areas.

Today, only 5 percent of the 53,000 members of the Air Line Pilots Association are women, and only 450 are airline captains. A deterrent for both men and women is the cost of training, which can range up to $100,000. Starting pay for regional or specialty airlines can be horrible. Although most female airline pilots today are based in the United States, women are making progress in other areas of the world, such as Asia.

Finding a job in aviation isn't impossible, but it does take dedication and a willingness to think creatively.

≣ PANCHO BARNES ≣

Stunt Flyer Extraordinaire

IN 1930, AN EARLY talking picture, *Hell's Angels*, featured two brothers with very different personalities who enlisted in Great Britain's Royal Air Force after World War I broke out. The film's producer, famed millionaire aviator Howard Hughes, considered the aerial battle scenes to be the most important. He wanted it to look authentic when the brothers destroyed a German munitions factory and then tried to escape the squadron of enemy fighters coming after them.

Hell's Angels was the top-grossing movie that year and eighth-highest-grossing film during the 1930s. *Hell's Angels* didn't use the green screens or computerized special effects that we see in movies today. Back then, filmmakers used actual pilots, like 29-year-old Pancho Barnes. As Hollywood's first stunt pilot,

Pancho worked in many Hollywood films, several of which were with Howard Hughes, who shared her love of flying.

From her work in films, Pancho founded one of the first unions in Hollywood, the Associated Motion Picture Pilots (AMPP). She wanted to make certain that stunt pilots received decent wages. She was the only female member of the AMPP for a long time.

———— • ————

Florence Leontine Lowe was born in 1901. The most important person during her childhood was her grandfather, Thaddeus Lowe, who created surveillance balloons and was in charge of the Union Army's Aeronautic Corps during the Civil War. Thaddeus Lowe shared his love of flight with his granddaughter and took her to her first air show when she was ten years old.

Noticing the mesmerized look in Florence's eyes, Thaddeus said, "When you grow up, everyone will be flying airplanes."

"Me too?"

"You too. You will be a great pilot someday."

Florence's parents, particularly her mother, spent much of their time attending society functions and parties. Florence didn't care about looking pretty or behaving as her mother wanted her to. Florence thought she was plain looking, and she preferred hunting or riding horses to dressing up. But her mischievous streak often got her into trouble. Trying to curb their daughter's wild tendencies, her parents sent her to Catholic school. Not only did Florence escape from the school, but she also escaped the country, riding to Tijuana, Mexico, on a horse.

The Lowes arranged for their daughter to marry an Episcopal minister, the Reverend Rankin Barnes. The marriage was unhappy from the start, even after the birth of a son. Once again, Florence left her life behind; this time she escaped on a banana boat. However, this boat was filled with guns and Mexican revolutionaries instead of bananas. The ship's helmsman was an American, Roger Chute.

Taking their leave from the revolutionaries, Roger and Florence traveled through Mexico for several months. Roger jokingly called her Pancho because she was disguised as a man. She liked the name and decided to keep it.

When she returned to the United States and her husband seven months later, Pancho was ready for a new adventure. Her parents had died, leaving her with an inheritance to spend. She asked Ben Caitlin, a veteran World War I pilot, to teach her to fly. He didn't want to teach a woman to fly, so he tried to scare her off by taking her on a demonstration flight filled with loops, twirls, and dives. Little did he know that the flight would make Pancho want to learn to fly even more.

Pancho was fearless in the air—sometimes even reckless. And she was just as mischievous in the air as she was on the ground. During her first solo, she repeatedly buzzed by her husband's church to disrupt his sermon.

Signed by Orville Wright, Pancho's pilot's license was number 3522; she soon bought a Travel Air Speedwing. Her friend, Bobbi Trout, told her about a women-only air race from Santa Monica to Cleveland. There was a lot of publicity about it because air officials and newspapers were saying that women shouldn't be allowed to race, that it was too dangerous. Pancho Barnes only had one thing to say to that: "Where do I sign up?"

Leading up to the Women's Air Derby, Pancho did what she did best, which was to shock people or make them laugh. She might be found with a cigar between her teeth or saying a vulgar word of two. When a newspaper reporter asked her how she balanced flying with her other duties, Pancho replied that flying was the perfect antidote to housework. She flew planes; she didn't do housework.

She took off with 19 other pilots, including Amelia Earhart. While she was trying to land in Pecos, Texas, a car dashed across the runway, causing her to crash. She was unable to complete the Powder Puff Derby, but she had a good time at the race, which was all that really mattered to her. Her motto was, "When you have a choice, choose happy."

Pancho bought a low-wing monoplane, a Travel Air Model R "Mystery Ship," for $13,000. It was only the second one ever made. With it, she began a barnstorming troupe called the Mystery Circus of the Air. On August 1, 1930, she took off in her Mystery Ship from the Van Nuys, California, airport. She pushed the speed to 196 miles per hour in sustained flight. She beat Earhart's speed record and assumed the title of the world's fastest woman. After that, she celebrated by flying to Mexico City, again a first for an American female pilot. She sold her circus in 1935.

In addition to her stunt pilot work, Pancho also worked for Lockheed as its first female test pilot. She performed maximum load tests on the Lockheed Vega, flying over the Mojave Desert.

Although Pancho liked to shock people, those who knew her realized that she had a big heart. She formed the Women's Air Reserve (WAR) to assist people in need of medical attention in times of disasters. The women who worked with WAR were trained in first aid and military maneuvers. Bobbi Trout helped Pancho, and they publicized WAR by flying around the Statue of Liberty with wingtip touching wingtip. Pancho and five of the women also promoted WAR in 1934 by flying cross-country.

Pancho's free spending, coupled with the Great Depression, drained her finances. With the last of her funds, she bought an 80-acre ranch in the Mojave Desert, north of Los Angeles. She started an airport and flight school but was forced to close the flight school when World War II began. Close to Edwards Air Force Base, her ranch became a popular place for air force personnel, aviators, and celebrities.

In 1947, General Jimmy Doolittle visited Pancho and went riding on a horse named Happy. After the ride, Doolittle told Pancho he had a "Happy bottom." Pancho loved it and renamed her ranch the Happy Bottom Riding Club. In addition to its own airport and horses for riding, the ranch had a bar, restaurant, hotel, swimming pool, dance hall, and rodeo.

Air force pilot Chuck Yeager was a regular at the Happy Bottom Riding Club. He explained that Pancho's popularity with

Breaking Mach 1

How many people heard the sonic boom coming from Edwards Air Force Base on October 14, 1947, is hard to say, but if Pancho heard it, she would have known that someone had just flown faster than the speed of sound. And she would have known that it was her buddy, fellow test pilot Chuck Yeager.

After World War II, Yeager continued serving in the new air force as a flight instructor and test pilot. He flew the rocket-powered Bell X-1 fighter plane and named the plane *Glamorous Glennis*, after his wife. On October 14, Yeager passed Mach 1, breaking the sound barrier. He soon arrived at the Happy Bottom Riding Club to claim the free steak dinner Pancho had promised him if he could do it. The celebration lasted until the early morning hours.

the people from Edwards Air Force Base was because "she loved pilots and shared our code."

Edwards Air Force Base needed to expand, but the only direction was through the Happy Bottom Riding Club. Pancho fought the air force to keep her land. When a fire broke out on Pancho's place in November 1953, she suspected it was arson but couldn't prove it. She soon gave up the ranch.

Pancho eventually made her peace with Edwards Air Force Base before she died in 1975. And the base remembers her each year by celebrating Pancho Barnes Day.

LEARN MORE

"Florence L. 'Pancho Barnes' Lowe" on the California State Military Museum website, http://www.militarymuseum .org/Barnes.html

The Happy Bottom Riding Club: The Life and Times of Pancho Barnes by Lauren Kessler (Random House, 2000)

Pancho Barnes Official Site, www.panchobarnes.com

Pancho: The Biography of Florence Lowe Barnes by Barbara Hunter Schultz (Little Buttes, 1996)

Powder Puff Derby of 1929: The True Story of the First Women's Cross-Country Air Race by Gene Nora Jessen (Sourcebooks, 2002)

LYNN RIPPELMEYER AND
≣ BEVERLY BURNS ≣

Airline Pilot Captains

ALTHOUGH WOMEN PILOTS HAVE proven their abilities in the skies in both peacetime and war, it took longer to convince commercial airlines that women could also pilot passenger aircraft. In 1934, Helen Richey became the first woman pilot hired by a regularly scheduled airline, but it would be almost forty years before the next woman piloted an airliner.

In the United States, the Department of Commerce regulated flying until the Federal Aviation Administration was formed in the 1950s. Until the 1970s, women were barred from both military and commercial flying. As soon as the ban was lifted, women began entering the commercial aviation industry. However, even though the government had given the OK, it still took time to convince commercial airlines that women could do the job.

Pilots must earn a commercial pilot's license to fly for airlines; that requires ground school and 200 to 300 hours of flight training. Commercial airline pilots must have earned at least a certificate for single-engine and multiengine aircraft, plus instrument ratings. Commercial airline pilots can find themselves working up to 14 to 16 hours straight and at all different hours. To captain an airliner, a pilot must have an Airline Transport Pilot certificate (ATP), which requires receiving a

Helen Richey

Helen Richey was an accomplished pilot; she had competed in all types of races from the time she earned her pilot's license in 1930. With a goal of flying mail and passengers, Helen earned her commercial pilot's license eight months after getting her private pilot's license. She applied for a copilot position with Central Airlines in December 1934. The president of the airline wanted the publicity that would come with hiring a competitive flyer who had just won the first Women's National Air Meet. Helen flew a 12-passenger "tri-motor" plane between Washington and Detroit, with stops in Pittsburgh and Cleveland. Male-led unions didn't think she belonged in the cockpit of an airline, and the Department of Commerce restricted her to three flights per month. Helen resigned in August 1935. She went on to fly a variety of planes for the British Air Transport Auxiliary before flying for the WASPs.

Patrice Clarke-Washington

According to Patrice Clarke-Washington, safety always comes first in her role as an airline captain. Many days are routine, but as soon as something unexpected happens, such as bad weather, she sometimes has to make difficult decisions. She is the first African American female captain of a major airline and a member of the Organization of Black Airline Pilots, a group of approximately 600 African American airline pilots. Of that number, perhaps ten or eleven are female.

Patrice was raised by her mother in a can-do atmosphere. When Patrice decided she wanted a career in travel, she decided she would be a pilot. After graduating from Embry-Riddle Aeronautical University, she went to work in the airline industry. Her first job was as a pilot for a small charter airline, Trans Island Airways. She moved to United Parcel Service as a flight engineer on the DC-8. She moved up to first office and then captain, a position she assumed in November 1984.

commercial pilot certificate, passing a written exam and an FAA flight exam, and racking up 1,500 pilot-in-command hours. The captain of a commercial airline is not only responsible for the airplane but also for the crew, passengers, and cargo.

Emily Warner became the next female airline pilot almost 40 years after Helen Richey. She started working with Frontier Airlines on January 29, 1973. American Airlines hired its first female pilot, Bonnie Tiburzi, a couple of months later. Later that year, Delta hired the company's first female pilot as well. In 1982, the first female jet captains in the United States were working for Piedmont Airlines. Two years later, Great Britain's first all-female airline crew flew passengers from England to Holland.

———•———

In 1984, women pilots rejoiced when two aviators demonstrated the capabilities of female pilots. Captain Lynn Rippelmeyer and Captain Beverly Burns both worked for People Express Airlines. On July 19, the two took off from New Jersey's Newark Interna tional Airport as the captains of Boeing 747s. At the time, the 747 was the ultimate airliner, often called a jumbo jet.

Lynn and Beverly were the first women to captain 747s. They flew in opposite directions for their historical flights. Beverly became the first woman to pilot a 747 cross-country to Los Angeles. Lynn did something similar to what Amelia Earhart had done fifty years earlier. She took the 747 across the Atlantic Ocean.

Lynn Rippelmeyer, from Illinois, began her aviation career as a flight attendant in 1972. At one point, she wasn't allowed to make announcements during flights. The airline believed that hearing a woman's voice during the flight would be upsetting for passengers.

Lynn began taking flying lessons and loved it. In fact, flying was addictive for her; when she wasn't doing it, she wanted to be. Within five years, she was part of the first all-female crew for a commercial airline. When Lynn landed her 747 with 470 passengers at Gatwick Airport in London, she became the first woman to fly a 747 commercial airliner across the Atlantic Ocean.

When the airline People Express became part of Texas Air, Lynn went along and became its second pilot. Later, the company became part of Continental Airlines. While she was with Continental, Lynn heard about a program called Medical Bridges. She saw the good things this medical charity was doing for others and began volunteering to fly medical supplies to clinics and hospitals in Honduras.

Like Lynn, Beverly also began her aviation career as a flight attendant. When talking about career choices with her high school counselor, Beverly mentioned that she would like a job in travel. The counselor recommended that Beverly be a stewardess, not a pilot.

She worked as a stewardess for American Airlines from 1971 to 1978. After overhearing a male first officer explain that women weren't smart enough to become airline pilot captains, Beverly promptly signed up for flying lessons. Her instructor, Robert Burns, had been taught by a former WASP who had made him promise to help a capable woman pilot break into the airline industry. When he met Beverly, it seemed like fate. The two later married.

Beverly's first job after receiving her license was as a charter pilot. She began as a first officer for People Express in 1981. Four years later, Beverly received the Amelia Earhart Award for her success as a commercial airline captain.

After 27 years of flying for airlines, Beverly retired with more than 25,000 flight hours. In addition to the 747, she has captained DC-9s, DC-10s, and Boeing aircraft 727s, 737s, 757s, 767s, and a Boeing 777. She was the first woman with Continental to captain a Boeing 777, and her first flight was from Houston, Texas, to London.

LEARN MORE

Great Women in Aviation #5: Captain Emily Warner—First Female Pilot Hired by a U.S. Scheduled Airline by Henry M. Holden (Black Hawk Publishing, 2012)

International Society of Women Airline Pilots website, www.iswap.org

Takeoff!: The Story of America's First Woman Pilot for a Major Airline by Bonnie Tiburzi (CreateSpace, 2010)

≣ WALLY FUNK ≣

Air Safety Investigator

WITH MORE THAN 18,500 hours in the air, Wally Funk has had almost every aviation-related job—flight instructor, transport pilot, commercial pilot, investigator, and more. CFI, AI, MEL, glider, IGI, GS, and air safety investigator—these are all certifications she has earned since she began flying at age 20.

———•———

Wally was born wanting to fly. She took her first test flight at age five when she jumped off her father's barn wearing a Superman cape. A bale of hay caught her. Growing up in Taos, New Mexico, in the 1940s and 1950s allowed her to spend lots of time outdoors trying out her athletic skills, whether she was running, skiing, or shooting. She received the Distinguished Rifleman's

Award at age 14. At the same time, she represented the south-western United States as a top female skier in slalom and down-hill races in United States competitions. When she was indoors, she built model airplanes.

Parental support came from her mother. Wally's mother recalled wanting to fly after taking a ride with a barnstormer when she was 16, but her father had told her she never would fly because she was female. Now that she had a daughter, Wally's mother didn't want her daughter's gender to limit what she could do. When Wally wasn't quite 21, she needed parental permission to participate in astronaut training. Wally's mother not only gave her permission, but she also drove her daughter to the week of tests in Albuquerque.

Several years earlier, after receiving her pilot's license at age 16, Wally was off to Stephens College in Columbia, Missouri. She enrolled in its aviation program and was first in her class of 24 fliers.

What's in a Name?

People often wonder if Wally's name is real. Yes and no. She was born Mary Wallace Funk. Like some people, she went by her middle name, but when the time came to put her name on her Christmas stocking, Wallace wouldn't fit. Not a problem—she just shortened it to Wally, and that's what it's been ever since. The Australian band Spiderbait liked her name so much that they used it in the name of one of their albums, *The Flight of Wally Funk*. Wally Funk is an unforgettable name for an unforgettable woman.

The Federal Aviation Administration

As more private airplanes and commercial airlines filled the skies, aviation became increasingly dangerous. The government assigned first the Department of Commerce and then the Civil Aeronautics Authority (CAA) the responsibility of enforcing air-traffic rules, certifying aircraft, and licensing pilots in the United States.

On June 30, 1956, a tragic accident between two passenger aircrafts occurred over the Grand Canyon, killing all 128 passengers on both planes. Within two years, Mike Monroney, Democratic senator from Oklahoma, introduced a bill to establish an independent agency to oversee civil aviation safety. The bill, after it was passed and signed into law, created the Federal Aviation Agency—later known as the Federal Aviation Administration and now better known as the FAA.

Wally returned to school, earning a bachelor of science degree in secondary education at Oklahoma State University with a minor in aviation. OSU's aviation program was popular, with up to 200 students per year, but Wally stuck out—not just because she was the only female but also because she had superior flying skills and a positive attitude. She loved competing against the boys. She was a member of the school's Flying Aggies, winning trophies at collegiate air meets. The team uniform was white coveralls, cowboy boots, and a cowboy hat. Wally earned even more pilot certifications while at college.

After graduating at age 20, she was refused employment at Continental and United Airlines. She said they told her they had

In 1966, president Lyndon Johnson introduced the Department of Transportation (DOT) to oversee all transportation policies, and the FAA became part of the Department of Transportation. Safety inspectors, air-traffic controllers, and safety marshals became important roles within the FAA. The FAA also ushered in modern technology to improve safety, including global positioning systems and other automated systems.

With the primary mission of advancing aviation safety, the FAA continues to perform research that leads to improvements in aviation. Excluding the terrorist attacks on September 11, 2001, there have been only 0.018 fatal accidents for every 100,000 planes that take off. (FAA duties changed soon after the 9/11 attacks. It continues to monitor safety and investigate accidents, but aviation security was taken over by the Transportation Security Administration (TSA), a department of Homeland Security.)

no women's bathrooms in their training facilities. Instead, she became the chief flight instructor—and the first female flight instructor—at Fort Sill, an army base in southwest Oklahoma. In more than 50 years of flight instruction, Wally has soloed more than a thousand students, putting them through various pilot certifications. She has also been honored with the FAA Gold Seal, an award given to flight instructors.

Wally's job as a flight instructor was just one of many firsts. As the first woman to complete the FAA General Aviation Operations Inspector Academy course in 1971, she learned about procedures for performing flight testing, certifying pilots, and handling accidents. This information became useful when she

Mercury 13 Astronaut

One day in 1960, Wally picked up the October issue of *Life* magazine. In it was a photo of a honey-blond pilot named Jerrie Cobb, who, according to the magazine, was proof that women should go into space. Wally decided she was going along with Jerrie Cobb. By the time she was 21, Wally had started the first phase of women's astronaut training. Although the women of the Mercury 13 scored well in all their testing—a few even did better than their male counterparts—Congress ruled that women didn't have the experience and abilities needed to be astronauts. This was 1963. A year later, the first woman, Valentina Tereshkova of the Soviet Union, went into space. Wally kept sending in her application to NASA. Twenty years later, American Sally Ride became the first American woman in space.

Wally is still waiting for her opportunity. She hoped it would be in 2013 on a private space flight, the Solaris X.

became the first woman investigator for the National Transportation Safety Board. Wally toured the world to lecture on safety training. She was the first woman to hold many positions within the FAA, including air safety investigator.

Wally retired from the National Transportation Safety Board in 1985 to devote her time to safety education. Today, she travels and makes presentations, including one she calls "How to Fly and Stay Alive." With all her work and training in safety investigations, Wally hopes that the more people know about air safety, the smaller the chances are that an accident will happen. Her goal is to make the already safe skies even safer.

In the late 1960s, Wally spent three years as a goodwill flying ambassador, traveling more than 80,000 miles as she visited 50 countries in Europe, Africa, and the Middle East.

When not working, Wally enters air races, including the Air Race Classic, Palms to Pines Race, and the Pacific Air Race. She flew into a first-place finish from San Diego to Santa Rosa, California, against 80 competitors. She also enjoys ballooning, hang gliding, and skydiving.

In 1985, Wally was inducted into the Women in Aviation International Pioneer Hall of Fame. Despite earning this great achievement, Wally hasn't stopped pushing herself. Today she looks forward to the day when she can have the ultimate experience: going to space. In the meantime, she remains as busy as ever. Living in Fort Worth, Texas, she flies almost every day. She has served as chief pilot at North Texas Aero airport. In 2010, she learned how to fly a Black Hawk helicopter. With 15 ratings and licenses and experience with more than 30 types of planes, she continues to lecture, teach flight training, and consult for aerospace companies. She has also remained active with the Ninety-Nines.

Wally is much in demand as a speaker. Her exuberant personality and quick laugh make her popular with audiences. Ask her to inspect a plane, and she'll whip out her "Wally stick" and check the prop for cracks. People remember what Wally Funk tells them.

LEARN MORE

Almost Astronauts: 13 Women Who Dared to Dream by Tanya Lee Stone and Margaret A. Weitekamp (Candlewick, 2009)

The Mercury 13: The True Story of Thirteen Women and the Dream of Space Flight by Martha Ackmann and Lynn Sherr (Random House, 2004)

"Wally Funk" on Ninety-Nines, Inc. International Organization of Women Pilots website, www.ninety -nines.org/index.cfm/wally_funk.htm

"Wally Funk" on Women Fly Resource Center website, http://womenaviators.org/WallyFunk.html

Wally Funk website, http://wallyfly.com

≣ PATTY WAGSTAFF ≣

Aerobatic Firefighter

THE AIRPLANE SOARS STRAIGHT up. It seems to freeze in the sky before it goes into a series of loops and barrel rolls, like the wildest roller coaster ever built. A white-gray jet stream shoots from the plane like a ribbon ready to be tied. Then the plane flips over, flying upside down.

The plane drops close to the ground in a feat of low-level extreme aerobatics. With one wrong move, it would crash. Other than the plane, the only sounds are the collective oohs and ahhs from the audience.

This scene typifies the life of Patty Wagstaff, who performs exciting aerial acrobatics for millions of people throughout the world. As a six-time member of the US Aerobatic Team, she has won gold, silver, and bronze medals in international competitions.

Patty was born in 1951 into an air force family in the United States, and they moved to Japan when she was nine years old. Her father was a 747 captain for Japan Air Lines, so she grew up around airplanes. (Her sister, Toni, would later fly a 727 for Continental Airlines.) Her father used to let her sit on his lap in the cockpit of the planes. When she was 10, she had her first exciting moment with an airplane: she got to take over the controls of her father's DC-6.

Patty's early life in Japan led to a love of travel as well. After traveling throughout Southeast Asia and Europe, she moved to a small boat and sailed the west coast of Australia.

Returning to the United States in 1979, Patty made the southwest Alaska town of Dillingham her home. She took a job that required her to travel to villages that were accessible only by air. But when the chartered plane she was riding in crashed on her first trip, she decided it was time for her to learn to fly. She learned on a Cessna 185 floatplane in Alaska's often-treacherous weather and terrain. While taking lessons, she met her future husband, Bob.

Since learning to fly, Patty has received other certifications, including commercial, instrument, multiengine, seaplane, and commercial helicopter ratings. She can fly anything from a World War II fighter to a jet. Patty also teaches flying and instrument rating to others.

Attending her first air show in 1983, Patty watched the aerobatics in awe. She was determined to learn how to perform those maneuvers herself. Within two years, she had landed a spot on the US Aerobatic Team. She liked how aerobatics demanded 100 percent of her concentration; she has described it as being one with the plane.

What Is Aerobatics?

Aerobatics is aerial acrobatics. Pilots perform complicated maneuvers with their airplanes. It is a type of flying that requires much skill and confidence. It's also very entertaining. One of the earliest female aerobatic performers was Betty Skelton, who began performing in 1947. She flew a hand-built plane to win the Feminine International Aerobatics Championships for three years in a row. She named her plane *Little Stinker*.

An aerobatics competition takes place on a playing field, or "box." A flyer must remain in bounds or be penalized. The judging for aerobatics is similar to that for gymnastics or figure skating. Each maneuver or figure receives a score of between 0 and 10, the best score. A k-factor rates the degree of difficulty. Each score is multiplied by the k-factor for the figure score. Then all the scores for each move are added up. The high score wins.

Aerobatic pilots start by competing in classical categories before moving on to a qualification program, freestyle routines, and unknowns. After each section, only the best aerobatic pilots remain in the competition.

Patty became the first female to win the National Aerobatic Championships in 1991. It was then that she realized that flying was a double-edged sword. As a woman, she was under more scrutiny. Determined to prove herself, she went on to win the competition two more times. Today, she is still the only woman to have won the National Aerobatic championships three times.

For this feat, she was honored by the Smithsonian's National Air and Space Museum. Her airplane, the Extra 260, is featured in the museum, right behind Amelia Earhart's airplane.

Patty's aerobatic career has spanned the globe; she has traveled to places such as Iceland and Russia, where she trained with the Russian aerobatic team. Her experience includes flight testing for aircraft manufacturers and working as a stunt pilot for film and television. Currently the only female member of the Motion Picture Pilots Association, Patty doubles for male and female actors. In television, she has done work for both educational television (on the Discovery Channel and the Learning Channel) and popular television (*Lois and Clark*). Movie work and commercials are also part of her stunt-flying resume.

Patty has also found a way to use her aviation skills and talent to give back. She regularly travels to East Africa to train antipoaching pilots in the Kenya Wildlife Service to help protect Kenya's wildlife. Elephants are particularly at risk because of the demand for ivory, and the most successful method of deterring poachers is air patrol. Since she started the training program, pilot accidents have decreased by half, and the elephant population has increased. The program is supported in part by the Charles A. and Anne Morrow Lindbergh Foundation. Charles Lindbergh was a supporter of wildlife and enjoyed visiting Africa.

After 12 years of winning practically every award for aerobatics, Patty retired from competing. She found a new way to use her skills: Patty joined Cal Fire as an aerial firefighter. The US Forest Service requires firefighting pilots to have 800 pilot-in-command flight hours, with 100 of those hours completed during the past year. Fire pilots must have ratings in multiengine flying, instrument rating, and commercial flying.

Aerial firefighting is a demanding profession. During the season, a pilot works six days on, one day off. You can be called out at any point and must be ready to fly.

As an air-attack pilot, Patty flies an OV-10 Bronco to fight fires in California. Flying through smoke and flames demands all her aerobatic skills and more. She and an air tactical group supervisor are often first on the scene, surveying the landscape and determining the best methods to attack a wildfire. They communicate their findings to ground firefighting crews and other air crews. Patty also broadcasts warnings to airports for other pilots to stay away. She hopes to one day be ready for tanker flying.

Tankers, which fly low to the ground, were first used to put out fires with water or chemical retardants in the 1950s. Old military planes were modified for this purpose. Tanker planes that were specifically developed to fight fires, like the Canadair CL-215, have features such as doors in the belly of the plane that drop water on fires. Some can even scoop up to 1,400 gallons (5,300 liters) of water from nearby lakes in seconds.

"Tanker flying is edgy," Patty explained in an interview, "because you are low and in the smoke in places you've never been before. Everything is totally different down there: trees sticking up everywhere, small flames, and no perspective. When there is a lot of wind, it can be really ugly too, but it's cool, totally cool! I love it."

At the peak of wildfire season, Patty may fly up to seven hours per day. The people of California depend on the shiny red-and-white airplanes that come to their rescue when wildfires strike. Patty's airplane and the tankers are kept ready to go. When the buzzers sound at the bases, the crews must quickly slide into their flight suits and be up in the sky in minutes.

Firefighting keeps her busy and on call for four to five months per year. Patty saves aerobatic air shows for after fire season. But whether performing for audiences or fighting fires, she gives flying everything she's got.

LEARN MORE

Aerial Firefighting by Wolfgang Jendsch (Schiffer Publishing, 2008)

Basic Aerobatics by Geza Szurovy and Mike Goulian (McGraw-Hill Professional, 1994)

Fire and Air: A Life on the Edge by Patty Wagstaff and Ann L. Cooper (Chicago Review Press, 1997)

"Patricia 'Patty' Wagstaff" on National Aviation Hall of Fame website, www.nationalaviation.org/wagstaff-patty

"Patty Wagstaff: Fire and Air" on Ninety-Nines, Inc. International Organization of Women Pilots website, www.ninety-nines.org/index.cfm/patty_wagstaff.htm

"Patty Wagstaff Interview and Flight" on YouTube, www.youtube.com/watch?v=Y4NJnyx4zAl

≣ INGRID PEDERSEN ≣

Polar Bush Pilot

ON JULY 29, 1963, Ingrid Pedersen took off from Fairbanks, Alaska, in a red-and-white Cessna 205, nicknamed the *Snow Goose*. Originally, she and her husband, Einar, were to leave in spring, but they had been delayed. She had her hands full trying to pilot the small plane over the North Pole. They had replaced four of the seats with extra fuel tanks for the 2,400-mile trip (3,900 kilometers) across the Arctic.

The fuel tanks, fuel, and emergency equipment added more than 700 pounds (320 kilograms) to the airplane. This weight made the back of the plane heavy, affecting the balance. Ingrid thought her *Snow Goose* was more like an overfilled goose. She compensated for the weight and balance by flying with the nose down for the first few hours.

But the extra weight also made the plane's high-pitched stall warning go off for almost an hour. Ingrid did her best to ignore it and focus on flying. When the landscape is all white as it is in the polar regions, pilots can become disoriented. Ellen Paneok, an Anchorage bush pilot, compared it to flying inside a milk bottle.

Einar stayed busy with navigating and taking pictures of the ice for his research. He had brought five cameras in addition to navigational equipment. Magnetic compasses are useless when flying over the North Pole, so Einar had to use other tools, including the sun. When he worked for Scandinavian Airlines, he had developed a system for polar navigation using grids, charts, and a sextant. One of his tools was a telescope-like gadget called a drift sight. When he placed it against the window of the plane, he could calculate the wind speed, which allowed him to evaluate how the wind affected the plane's speed.

When enough fuel had burned off, the *Snow Goose* became easier to handle. Ingrid noticed a blue ice island known as T-3. Ice

The North Pole

The Arctic area, including the North Pole, was covered with ice year round when Ingrid Pedersen made her historic journey. Today, the area has adopted seasonal fluctuations due to climate change. In winter, the average temperature is –29° F (–34° C). But the summer averages 32° F (0° C). Since the 1970s, the arctic sea ice has been decreasing approximately 12 percent each year. As a result of climate change, the Arctic is warming almost twice as fast as the rest of the planet.

islands or icebergs are classified according to shape or size. T-3 has a tabular shape, with steep sides and a flat top like a plateau. Ingrid thought the island, though beautiful, looked lonely in the middle of the Arctic Ocean, covered with a layer of shifting ice.

When Ingrid got close to Spitsbergen, the largest of the populated Norwegian islands that border the Arctic Ocean, it became obvious that the *Snow Goose* was collecting too much ice. She dropped the plane to about 500 feet (150 meters) to melt the ice, watching as chunks of it fell off.

After 21 hours of flying, the Pedersens landed on Station Nord in Greenland. After a rest, they flew on to Bodo, Norway, another 11 hours away, making Ingrid the first woman to fly successfully over the North Pole.

For her achievement, Ingrid received the Amelia Earhart Medal from the Alaska Ninety-Nines and a Gold Plaque from the Royal Swedish Aero Club. Although her record flight was big news in Alaska and the countries of Scandinavia, where she was from, it didn't get a lot of attention in other locations. Since the dawn of aviation, there had been many first flights.

People in Alaska, particularly pilots, know how dangerous flying over the North Pole can be. It's a long flight during which traditional navigation doesn't work. On clear days, the line of the horizon aids pilots by breaking up the white landscape. But hazardous weather can occur at any time and create even worse whiteout conditions. Modern navigational aids such as GPS help, but it remains a difficult trip.

———•———

Ingrid was born in 1933 in Stockholm, Sweden. Being a pilot was not something she dreamed of while growing up. Instead, she wanted to see wild animals and have adventures in Africa.

But then she met Einar Pedersen, whom she called "the Polar Professor." He was a polar navigator who studied polar ice. His apartment walls were decorated with photographs of wild animals, such as polar bears and seals. In spite of herself, Ingrid found herself drawn to the polar region.

Einar dared Ingrid to learn to fly. Unable to resist the challenge, she began taking flight lessons in February 1957. Her husband called her a natural-born pilot. After soloing in May, she earned her license in June. She was the 13th woman in Sweden to receive a pilot's license.

After the two married, Einar was transferred to Anchorage for an 18-month rotation by Scandinavian Airlines. Ingrid obtained commercial, instrument, and airline-transport ratings. In 1959 they began talking about making the polar flight. Finally, as 1963 approached, they decided it was now or never.

After the historic flight, they returned to Europe for a while. Ingrid flew commercially through the Arctic as a bush pilot, taking researchers, miners, and supplies to remote locations. During this time, she was frequently the first woman pilot to complete many of the routes she flew. Ingrid is credited with ten first flights, mainly in the polar region.

During the mid-1970s, the Norwegian Polar Institute hired the Pedersens to place meteorological buoys on the drift ice to collect data. The institute studies the Arctic region and manages the environmental needs in the region. Ingrid taught herself to land a Cessna on drift ice in the Arctic Ocean. Not many pilots can successfully land on moving, icy runways. The Pedersens landed in seven different polar ice locations to set up the buoys that would measure ice drift. On one landing, one of the plane's skis got stuck, but they were able eventually to break free.

The Pedersens returned to Alaska in 1979. Ingrid continued piloting commercial flights from Skagway and also became a flight instructor in Anchorage. She became a US citizen in 1985 and volunteered at the Alaska Aviation Heritage Museum. Ten years later, she published a book about flying in the Arctic. The title translates to "perfume and motor oil."

Today, airliners fly over the North Pole; doing so cuts significant time off routes to Scandinavian countries, Russia, and parts of Asia. But for small planes, this can still be a hazardous trip. Since Ingrid made her flight, other women have made the trip and experienced both the joys and problems. Polly Vacher is one of those women. With a goal of starting a scholarship for disabled pilots, she set out to fly around the globe over both the North and South Poles. When she was flying over the North Pole, her engine stalled. Although she was able to get it started again, the dangers of a crash and small chances of survival made this experienced pilot more than a little nervous.

Flying over the North Pole was almost unheard of, for male or female pilots, when Ingrid Pedersen made her historic journey. She continued flying in the harsh polar region for many years. For Ingrid, life as a polar aviator meant never a dull moment.

LEARN MORE

Flying the Arctic by Captain George H. Wilkins (Kessinger Publishing, 2004)

The Ice Pilots: Flying with the Mavericks of the Great White North by Michael Vlessides (Douglas and McIntyre, 2011)

PART V

Making a Difference

Women pilots have made their mark in all types of flying: competitive, military, and commercial. Some female pilots quit flying when they were denied the flying careers they were best suited to. Others used their skills and interest in flying to make a difference in the lives of others.

World War II was a frightening time; people worried about their security. It was also a time when people began to see how aviation could benefit others. One week before the attack on Pearl Harbor, the Civil Air Patrol (CAP) was created as an aviation group that would do just that. More than 150,000 volunteers logged more than 500,000 flying hours. CAP volunteers delivered cargo and mail to air bases, monitored the country's borders and provided civil defense. CAP pilots spent 46,725 hours towing targets to provide training for gunners and searchlight operators. They even sank two enemy submarines.

Women were allowed to fly in noncombat zones, often as couriers for the CAP. At a time when women had a difficult time getting accepted in the CAP, Willa Brown became the first African American to serve as an officer in the Civil Air Patrol. She was the Chicago coordinator and leader of the first integrated unit. Ruth Nichols also served in the CAP as a lieutenant colonel. By the end of World War II, reportedly 20 percent of the Civil Air Patrol was female.

People donate their time and skills to make the world a better place. Organizations such as the Peace Corps and UNICEF provide education, training, and support throughout the world. Doctors Without Borders, Red Cross, and Medical Missions, Inc. provide health care. All of these groups need pilots, as do environmental and religious groups that serve others.

Twenty-three-year-old Patricia Mawuli is not only one of Ghana's youngest pilots; she is also the country's first female

The Civil Air Patrol Today

During World War II, people wondered why the Civil Air Patrol couldn't continue after the war was over. In 1946, president Harry Truman designated the CAP a nonprofit charity. Two years later, Congress passed a law making the CAP an auxiliary of the US Air Force. The CAP continues to provide disaster relief and emergency service, flying for organizations such as the Red Cross and the Federal Emergency Management Agency (FEMA). CAP volunteers also fly more than 85 percent of the search-and-rescue missions in the continental United States.

Two other functions of CAP are aerospace education and a cadet program. The aerospace program focuses on educating CAP volunteers and the public. The cadet program provides aeronautic education, leadership training, and physical fitness instruction to youth from ages 12 to 21.

pilot. She teaches at Ghana's Aviation and Technology Academy. In her free time, she volunteers with Medicine on the Move, an organization that delivers medical services to Ghana's rural population. Patricia delivers supplies and doctors across her country. She also flies over villages and drops educational pamphlets about health issues such as malaria.

Flying charities, such as Flight Charities, Inc., transport people and supplies to medical facilities and provide assistance after natural disasters occur. Air Charity Network, which has more than 7,500 volunteer pilots, also provides flights for medical emergencies, disaster response, and travel for military personnel. The Aircraft Owners and Pilots Association (AOPA) oversees and regulates many charitable flights.

Other flying charities, such as Angel Flight, work under the Air Care Alliance. These organizations provide free air transportation for charitable or nonemergency medical needs. They also transport blood for the Red Cross and the Oklahoma Blood Institute in emergencies. Each pilot must have both a private pilot's license and a medical certificate as well. The costs of these flights are primarily covered by the pilots themselves, who use their own airplanes and pay for their own operating expenses. Based in Tulsa, Oklahoma, Angel Flight primarily serves the central United States but coordinates with other similar services when longer flights are needed—for example, to specialty hospitals.

Other flying charities and pilots provide service in other countries, which can be challenging, with hostile terrain and a lack of runways. Pilots carry food, medicine, and immunizations—all of which can save lives. Sometimes a pilot might be the difference between people living or dying.

Yet this aspect of the job is where the reward comes from, knowing one's flying skills are making a difference in the lives of others. Women pilots make a difference whether they volunteer

Air Marking

The next time you go flying, look down. If you see arrows, compasses, or airport names, you are seeing the work of volunteers. The National Air Marking Program was started as a government program under the jurisdiction of the Bureau of Air Commerce National Advisory Committee for Aeronautics (which later became NASA). Phoebe Omlie, a charter member of the Ninety-Nines, planned the program and put it into action in the 1930s. At the time, most planes did not have radios, and no one had GPS.

After thousands of directional aids were painted in the 1930s, the markers were blacked out during World War II so as not to serve as targets for enemy bombing. After the war ended, Blanche Noyes headed the program to restore the markers and add even more. Because this was no longer part of a federal program, Blanche gained financial support from civic groups around the country to pay for the air-marking supplies.

Today's fellow Ninety-Nines take care of air marking on a voluntary basis. They paint airport names and directional compass roses, sometimes up to 50 feet (15 meters) long, on rooftops and the ground so that pilots can see them from the air.

to teach Girl Scouts how to fly, work on one of the Ninety-Nine's many projects, or volunteer for some other organization. Aviation makes a difference in everyone's life.

Ninety-Nines members have a long history of giving back. Carole Cary-Hopson has mentored at-risk girls in the Eagle

Flight Squadron in New Jersey. Eagle Flight Squadron is a non-profit youth organization that encourages aviation skills. Cary-Hopson worked with one girl who wanted to fly so much that she would take two buses and a train to get to the meetings. That's dedication—and proof of the many ways that aviation changes lives.

⫸ RUTH NICHOLS ⫷

Relief Wings in Times of Disaster

RUTH NICHOLS, A PIONEER AVIATOR with dozens of records to her name, saw her world turned upside down by World War II. She began to look at aviation differently. Instead of seeing aviation as a competition to fly faster, higher, and farther than anyone else, Ruth realized that planes could used to help others. With their machines, pilots could give people in needy communities a better chance at surviving by bringing them the goods they lacked or transporting them quickly to medical facilities.

She joined the Civil Air Patrol and served as a lieutenant colonel. She saw how the organization accomplished many good things for the war effort, but she believed more could be done.

In 1940, Ruth established Relief Wings as a flying ambulance to help during disasters. When presenting her plan to government officials and the public, Ruth explained how planes could be used for mercy missions. Airplanes could go where ambulances couldn't. And if the nearest medical facility was far away, a plane could get there faster.

She recommended twin-motor planes capable of flying through any type of weather. The planes had to be large enough to carry patients on stretchers if needed, plus medical personnel, including a doctor and nurse. Relief Wings later became a service of the Civil Air Patrol, and Ruth continued as an advisor to the air ambulance missions.

When the war ended, Ruth continued volunteering her time. She worked on missions with UNICEF, including an around-the-world tour for the International Children's Emergency Fund in 1949. On that trip, the large, four-engine airline carrying Ruth and 56 others overshot its refueling stop—then it ran out of gas and crashed into the North Sea.

It was nighttime. The water was freezing. Being weighted down with wet clothes made swimming almost impossible. In the moonlight, Ruth spotted an upside-down 10-person raft with 14 of her people hanging on. She made her way to it. The water was rough, causing the raft to dip. At some point, the group was able to tip it over and get inside. The 15 people crowded together, trying to get warm; an unconscious man lay in Ruth's lap. She started singing hymns, calming everyone down.

When dawn came, the group counted 11 search planes in the sky. They circled nearby but didn't spot them. Finally, a 12th plane saw them, and they were rescued. Nine of the original 57 lost their lives.

Ruth was involved with other humanitarian causes as well, including her work with organizations such as Save the Children, the United Hospital Fund, and the National Nephrosis Foundation.

Air Ambulances

Although Ruth Nichols is to be commended for introducing and starting air ambulance services in the United States, she wasn't the first. Air ambulances have been around longer than airplanes!

The first air ambulances appeared in 1870 during the Franco-Prussian War. In this case, the ambulances were hot-air balloons, and they moved injured soldiers to hospitals. In 1910, attempts were made to use airplanes as ambulances, but airplanes were still so relatively new and fragile that often they crashed before reaching hospitals. Although some countries had isolated success with using airplanes as ambulances during World War I, many of the details still hadn't been worked out. The United States found that the planes couldn't fit stretchers, and the open cockpit was often harmful to the patients. Bigger planes, particularly those modified to be used as ambulances, were created for use during the 1936–1939 Spanish Civil War. During the Korean War, which lasted from 1950 to 1953, helicopters began serving as air ambulances.

Civil air ambulances didn't begin to grow until after World War II. The first nonmilitary air ambulance in North America was in Saskatchewan, Canada. In 1947, the first FAA-certified air ambulance in the United States was developed in Los Angeles, California.

Born in New York City in 1901, Ruth Rowland Nichols came
from a well-off family. Her mother was the daughter of a
Quaker minister. Ruth said she received her quiet faith from her
mother and grandfather; meanwhile, her attitude and personality seemed to come from her father. He was a successful busi-
nessman and a member of the New York Stock Exchange. As
one of Teddy Roosevelt's Rough Riders, Ruth's father believed
she should try everything once, and if she failed, she was to get
back up and try again. Although Ruth may have been born to
money and privilege, she was also a determined young woman.

Ruth attended private schools while growing up. When
she graduated from high school—the Miss Masters' School in
Dobbs Ferry, New York—her father arranged an airplane ride
with Eddie Stinson, a World War I pilot and brother to the Stinson sisters, who were also aviators. Ruth was very excited. Stinson was a hero of hers. But during the flight in a World War
I Jenny, Stinson did a loop-the-loop, a big circle in the air that
briefly involves flying upside down. Ruth was scared to death
and unable to enjoy the rest of the flight.

But Ruth's response, when faced with fear, was to confront
it. She did this by taking flying lessons while attending college. When she graduated from Wellesley College in 1924, she
promptly took the test for her pilot's license. She passed, becoming the first New York woman pilot and the second woman
licensed by the Department of Commerce.

Conquering her fear led to a love of flying. Despite her parents wanting her to settle down as a proper young woman of
the times, she insisted on flying and even learned to fly and fix
a Curtiss Seagull, a seaplane. Ruth became the first female seaplane pilot in the United States. No other female pilot of her generation could fly as many types of aircraft as she could. Over the
course of her flying career, she flew 71 different kinds of aircraft

from 50 different manufacturers. She earned 12 different ratings in everything from monoplanes to supersonic jets.

In January 1928, Ruth flew a Fairchild FC-2 from New York to Miami with Harry Rogers, the owner of an airline. As the first flight of its kind, the trip received a lot of publicity and led the newspapers to christen Ruth "the Flying Debutante."

In her purple flying suit, flying helmet, scarf, and goggles, Ruth became a familiar sight in newspapers and on airfields. This was especially true in 1929, when she landed in all 48 states (Alaska and Hawaii weren't states yet) on a promotional tour for aviation country clubs.

As one of the original Ninety-Nines, Ruth joined her fellow female aviators at the Women's Air Derby and National Air Race. She set a women's transcontinental record flying from New York to Los Angeles in 16 hours, 59 minutes, and 30 seconds. She shaved almost four hours off that time on the return trip.

The International League of Aviators honored two women in 1931 for their accomplishments in the advancement of aviation. They included French flier Maryse Bastié, for a 1,800-mile (2,900 kilometer) record-breaking flight from France to Russia, and Ruth Nichols, for her speed and altitude records.

Ruth prepared to be the first female to fly solo across the Atlantic Ocean to Paris. Her plane was said to be three times as powerful as Lindbergh's *Spirit of St. Louis*, capable of speeds 50 to 75 miles per hour (80 to 120 kilometers per hour) faster than Lindbergh's aircraft. The red monoplane, which belonged to Crosley Radio Corporation, was the same red monoplane she had set records in. One of those records was for speed—210 miles per hour (340 kilometers per hour). Briefly, she set another for altitude, but Elinor Smith soon broke it. Speed records were Ruth's favorite, and she tried to close in on male records.

Ruth's first attempt as the first woman to pilot solo across the Atlantic led to a crash in Newfoundland during the first leg of her trip. Blinded by the sun, she overshot the runway. The plane tipped at its nose. She fractured five of her vertebrae, and while she was recovering from this serious injury, another female aviator, Amelia Earhart, captured the record, becoming the first woman to fly solo across the Atlantic.

Disappointed, Ruth threw herself into making other records. In one of her first flights after her accident, she set a woman's distance record of 1,977 miles (3,181 kilometers). For some of the first races, she wore a steel corset due to her spinal injury. At one point, she had to leap out of a burning airplane after a fuel leak started a fire.

By Ruth's count, she had been in 55 accidents, and five of those were "major crack-ups." But Ruth didn't let injury or accidents deter her. She went on to fly higher than any woman in the world at 28,743 feet (8,767 meters). The next month, she set a speed record of 210.6 miles (338.9 kilometers) per hour. By 1931, Ruth was the first woman to simultaneously hold three international records for altitude, speed, and long distance.

When flying opportunities were curtailed during World War II, Ruth used her talents for humanitarian causes. She also worked as the director of a major aviation company, the Fairchild Airplane Manufacturing Corporation.

Ruth Nichols died on September 25, 1960. Part of the propeller from her Lockheed Vega is displayed in the Golden Age of Flight gallery at the National Air and Space Museum. Two years before she died, she set another record as a copilot in the supersonic Air Force TF-102A Delta Dagger. She flew at 51,000 feet (15,600 meters) and 1,000 miles per hour (1,600 kilometers per hour)—faster than any woman in the world.

According to Ruth, "It takes special kinds of pilots to break frontiers, and in spite of the loss of everything, you can't clip the wings of their hearts." She left a mark on women's aviation and demonstrated how aviation could help others.

LEARN MORE

"Ruth Nichols" on Smithsonian National Air and Space Museum website, http://airandspace.si.edu/explore-and -learn/topics/women/Nichols.cfm

"Ruth Nichols" on National Aviation Hall of Fame website, www.nationalaviation.org/nichols-ruth

⋙ FAY GILLIS WELLS ⋘

Promoting World
Friendship through Flying

FAY GILLIS WELLS BELIEVED that aviation was capable of making the world a better place. With the goal of "world friendship through flying," she led efforts to establish the International Forest of Friendship in Amelia Earhart's hometown of Atchison, Kansas. Amelia once said, "You haven't seen a tree until you've seen its shadow from the sky."

Located outside of Atchison overlooking Lake Warnock, the International Forest of Friendship is a beautiful place. It was created in 1976 as a bicentennial gift to the United States. After almost forty years, many of the trees have become quite large.

The forest is made up of trees from every location where a member of the Ninety-Nines has lived—all 50 states in the United States and 35 countries. There are trees from George

Washington's Mount Vernon and the farm that belonged to Amelia Earhart's grandfather. A very special tree is the Moon Tree, grown from a seed that went to the moon with astronauts on Apollo 14. The names of astronauts who have died on duty are engraved around the tree, including the seven astronauts who died in the space shuttle *Challenger* in 1986.

Memory Lane, a five-foot-wide sidewalk, winds through the forest. The beginning is marked with a plaque inscribed with Joyce Kilmer's poem "Trees." Along the path are more than 900 granite plaques honoring great names in aviation: Amelia Earhart, Charles Lindbergh, Harriet Quimby, Bobbi Trout, Ida Van Smith, Wiley Post, Patty Wagstaff, Chuck Yeager, Sally Ride, and many more. Each year, more honorees are inducted into the International Forest of Friends.

A life-size statue of Amelia Earhart looks out over the trees. Nearby is a gazebo, the Fay Gillis Wells Gazebo, dedicated in 1991. It's a good place to remember an important woman in aviation.

———•———

It was a sunny afternoon on the first day of September 1929. Twenty-year-old Fay Gillis was flying in a new plane that her instructor was testing. She had been taking lessons for a month and had just soloed the day before. She was hoping to experience some aerobatic flying with her instructor in the new plane.

Suddenly, the biplane began to break apart over Long Island Sound. The tail and the wings vibrated and then fell off. It flipped over, and Fay heard her instructor yelling at her to jump. She struggled to free herself from the seatbelt. As soon as she was free, she fell. She began looking for the rip cord that would release the parachute and save her life. Curtiss Flying School required everyone to wear a parachute up in the air. They were told put their hand on the rip cord and jump clear of the plane. It was important to count to ten before pulling the cord so that the parachute didn't hit the plane.

But Fay spent precious time just trying to find her rip cord. When she finally found it, she pulled hard, knowing she was too close to the ground. She braced herself for impact. But the hard fall to the ground never happened. Instead, Fay felt herself swinging in the air. Her parachute had caught in a tree.

A fire truck from the airfield came to release her from the branches. They and the parachute had saved her life. The pilot instructor wasn't so lucky; he later died from injuries from the accident. The parachute earned Fay a place as one of the first women members of the Caterpillar Club, a club for people who had been saved by parachuting after bailing out of airplanes.

The incident also brought Fay fame and a job—all before her 21st birthday. Glenn Curtiss offered her a job selling and demonstrating airplanes for Curtiss Aviation. She was the first woman it had ever hired for this position, and it allowed her to meet other aviators. A month later, she earned pilot's license number 9497 at Curtiss Flying Service in Valley Stream. This location was also where the Ninety-Nines organization was launched four days later by women aviators Fay had met. Fay, who had just flown in, was wearing coveralls for the first meeting on November 2. She became a charter member of the Ninety-Nines.

———•———

Helen Fay Gillis was born in Minneapolis, Minnesota, on October 15, 1908. She soon became known as Fay. Her father's profession as a mining engineer meant frequent moves, because he supervised the building of electrolytic zinc plants. Moving was an adventure for the Gillis family, particularly for Fay and her sister, Beth.

The two sisters were very close. Fay skipped a grade in school and ended up being in the same grade as Beth. Fay most enjoyed writing while in school. She was a reporter for her high school newspaper. Unfortunately, when the girls were juniors in high school, their mother died.

Both girls attended Michigan State University. Beth decided to study psychology and sociology, but Fay didn't know what to study. Restless, she moved to New York to take flying lessons at the Curtiss Flying School in Long Island, New York. Airplanes fascinated her. The slim, blue-eyed brunette also still had writing in her blood, so after she got her pilot's license, she began working as a journalist. Aviation was one of her favorite topics. When her father's business moved to the Soviet Union, Fay joined him in September 1930. Although she continued writing about aviation, she became a foreign correspondent too, writing for the *New York Herald Tribune* and the *New York Times*.

She didn't stop flying, though. Fay was the first foreigner to own a glider in the Soviet Union and the first American woman to fly Soviet civil aircraft. Her reputation as an expert aviator opened doors. Aviator Wiley Post arranged for her to coordinate landing and refueling stops for him in the Soviet Union during his 1933 record flight around the world. Wiley promised Fay that she could come along on his next adventure.

But when the time came for the trip to begin, Fay had to turn it down. In 1935, she chose instead to elope with a dashing journalist, Linton Wells. She would remember the decision for the rest of her life: Humorist Will Rogers took her place on Wiley's plane, but the two died upon takeoff in Point Barrow, Alaska.

Fay and Linton honeymooned in Ethiopia, where the two journalists covered the country's invasion by Italy from 1935 to 1936. Sometimes their bylines appeared side by side in the newspaper. They led an exciting life. Some people even believed she was a spy. When the Wells couple returned to the United States, they lived and worked for a time in Hollywood, covering the expanding movie industry. Fay often took her pet leopard, Snooks, on interviews.

After taking a break to raise her son, Fay returned to journalism as the first woman broadcast correspondent to cover US presidents Lyndon Johnson, Richard Nixon, Gerald Ford, and Jimmy Carter. As part of the White House press corps, she traveled to Vietnam and China.

Fay never forgot her devotion to aviation and the Ninety-Nines. Because of her efforts, the organization grew throughout

Eleven-Year-Old Writes
Fay Gillis Wells Biography

In 1997, eleven-year-old Sara Rimmerman met Fay Gillis Wells when Fay came to talk at Sara's Kansas school. Sara's sister, Rachel, had met the 90-year-old aviation journalist at a school assembly and couldn't wait to introduce Fay to her sister and mother. A small group met for tea, where Fay told wonderful stories about her life. They learned that no one had written a book about Fay. So the group decided that Sara, a fifth grader who loved to write, would tell Fay's story. After two years of interviewing, researching, and writing, Sara's book was published in 1999. It was called *Hidden Heroine* and told how Fay earned a pilot's license, lived in Russia, and became friends with Amelia Earhart.

the world, expanding to more than 3,000 members in 30 countries. She spearheaded efforts to bring women pilots together.

Fay honored her friend Amelia Earhart by creating a scholarship in her name in the 1940s. In the early 1960s, she worked to get the US Postal Service to honor Amelia Earhart's birthday by releasing an airmail stamp on her birthday. But that wasn't all. After her successful campaign for the stamp, she and other Ninety-Nines members gathered in Atchison and used the stamp on thousands of envelopes. The first of those canceled stamps, known as first-day covers, are the most coveted and therefore the most valuable. First-day covers were flown to almost every state capital in the United States and sold with proceeds going to the Amelia Earhart Memorial Scholarship fund.

Seventy years after receiving her pilot license, Fay was still flying—she even landed a plane on her 92nd birthday. Her one regret in life was that she hadn't been able to fly in space. Instead, she was part of a committee that selected the first journalist to go to space. It was the next best thing for this aviator journalist.

Fay died in December 2002 at the age of 94. She was active until the end, devoting her time and energy to other women aviators.

LEARN MORE

"Fay Gillis Wells" at the Women Fly Resource Center Women Pilots website, http://womenaviators.org/Fay.html

Fay Gillis Wells in the Air and On the Air by Lillian Brinnon and Howard Fried (Woodfield Press, 2002)

"Fay Gillis Wells" on the Ninety-Nines International Organization of Women Pilots website, www.ninety-nines.org/index.cfm/fay_gillis_wells.htm

Hidden Heroine—Fay Gillis Wells by Sara Rimmerman (Zeus Enterprises, 1999)

International Forest of Friendship website, http://ifof.org

≣ JENNIFER MURRAY ≣

Helicopter Flying for Charity

WHAT COULD MAKE A helicopter pilot—with injuries from a crash in freezing temperatures—want to get back in the helicopter to do it all over again? If you're 66-year-old Jennifer Murray, you're someone who enjoys a challenge. Many of her trips benefit charities. Her world-record trip around the world and over both the North and South Poles benefitted SOS Children's Villages, an organization that provides a family atmosphere for orphaned children.

Jennifer Murray and Colin Bodill set records on their own before meeting each other. Colin, a daredevil microlight flier since 1975, had won several British championships and a 1997 world championship. The two pilots started talking about circling the globe by crossing both the North and South Poles.

After three years of planning, their helicopter took off from New York on October 22, 2003. They flew along the east coast of both North and South America, alternating flying and navigating duties each day.

One of the most frightening sections of the trip was crossing the Drake Passage, the icy 540-mile (870 kilometer) body of water between South America and Antarctica. But they made it, becoming the first to fly a single-engine helicopter over the Drake Passage.

They set another record as the first civilian single-engine helicopter to reach the South Pole. The milestone was particularly special, as the date marked the 100th anniversary of the Wright brothers' first flight.

Antarctica is a particularly dangerous place to be. About 50 percent larger than the United States, it is always covered in snow. It is also the windiest place on Earth. On day 58 of their trip, a blizzard hit, making visibility nonexistent. Jennifer and Colin knew they had to land and wait out the storm, but because they could not see the landscape, they had to rely solely on their instruments. They crashed on the ice sheets of Antarctica; both pilots were injured. Colin had a broken back and internal bleeding. Jennifer sustained cracked ribs, cuts, and a dislocated elbow, and she went into shock. They knew they couldn't survive in the Antarctic cold of –50° C (–58° F) for long. At first, they lay next to the tangled metal they had flown. Finally, Colin was able to erect a tent to provide them with some protection from the elements. Jennifer said lying inside the tent was like being in a bowl of milk.

Before leaving on the trip, Jennifer and Colin had gotten a piece of new technology installed in their helicopter, a type of GPS/emergency response system called the D1000 tracker. When they crashed, the box called its emergency number, which connected to the manufacturers of the system. The manufacturers had the number to the base camp, approximately 200 miles (320 kilometers) from the crash site. The D1000 tracker was able to give Jennifer and Colin's location within 50 yards (45 meters).

The injured pilots heard a small plane fly over, but they knew that with the whiteout conditions, they couldn't be seen. The rescue plane landed near the coordinates and found Jennifer and Colin. The rescuers first took the two injured pilots to base, where they waited for further transportation. Even though they were in the middle of nowhere, Jennifer and Colin were able to get to a hospital less than 24 hours after they crashed.

On December 6, 2006, they made another attempt because, as Jennifer said, "You haven't failed until you stop trying." This time, Fort Worth, Texas, was the starting and finishing line. The day boasted blue skies and sunshine and a crowd of about 200 people to see Jennifer and Colin—the Polar First team—off on their journey.

Once again, they headed south along Central America. The first few days were met with route changes to avoid flying in bad weather. Even though they had crossed the Drake Passage before, Jennifer said she worried about the hostile body of water. They crossed it on December 30 and, for a change, had good weather awaiting them—for a few days at least.

The winds were particularly fierce, and they found themselves grounded for several days. They stayed in tents and abandoned huts at the Carvajal base. They weren't very welcome, though; a group of elephant seals took a disliking to the Polar First team, snapping at them.

There wasn't much to do except wait for the weather to clear. Jennifer and Colin get along well, except when it comes to music. Jennifer enjoys listening to classical music; Colin prefers anything else.

After the weather cleared, they took off for the site of their previous helicopter crash. Although the wrecked machine had been hauled off to a landfill, Colin still had the key, and the two buried it there. Although visiting the crash site and saying goodbye was emotional, the experience gave them closure.

The trip across Antarctica was almost entirely dictated by the weather. A hint of blue in the sky would send the pilots scurrying to pack up. Even when visibility was good with clear skies, they had to deal with strong headwinds. The higher their altitude, the greater the winds. But if they flew too low, they burned more fuel. Still, they usually found an altitude that worked out.

They crossed the Drake Passage again; this stage was shorter than anticipated due to strong tailwinds that put them back in Chile. They had survived the South Pole. Now it was time for the North Pole.

They approached the Arctic region in April. Jennifer admitted to having nerves, though this was mainly due to fear of the unknown. But flying over the North Pole was also similar to navigating over Antarctica in that they were constantly looking for windows of good weather. They found them and were on their way.

The red Bell 407 helicopter made the around-the-world flight from pole to pole in 170 days, 22 hours, 47 minutes, and 17 seconds; they reached the place they started, Fort Worth, on May 24, 2007. The amazing sights included two of the coldest places on Earth, as well as some of the hottest too. They refueled 101 times in 26 countries for the 32,206-mile (51,819 kilometer) trip.

The helicopter used on the world trip made a final trip to the Smithsonian National Air and Space Museum. Jennifer has been awarded both a silver medal and the Britannia Trophy by the Royal Aero Club. She's also a two-time Guinness World Record holder.

A trip like this takes a huge amount of preparation. Fueling stations and airports aren't very plentiful at either polar region, so Jennifer and Colin had to have fuel stored in remote locations. Fortunately, the woman who set the Guinness World Record in 1997 for flying the globe in a helicopter knew how to plan ahead.

———•———

Jennifer was born in Providence, Rhode Island, in 1940. Although she may have been born in the United States, her heart belongs to Great Britain. Her British father and American mother returned to England when she was four years old. She went to school there and graduated with a degree in textile design. In between working as a textile designer, she married, raised three children, and traveled the globe. She had a nose for adventure, whether it was trekking in Nepal or running a marathon.

Flying, however, wasn't one of the adventures that she ever considered. In fact, she didn't think about flying until she was 54. Her husband bought half a share in a helicopter. Jennifer said he told her that she had better learn to fly it because he didn't have time. Despite being asked if she wanted the "wives" course, which was little more than a helicopter tour, Jennifer signed up for helicopter training at flight school, and she found that she rather enjoyed it.

Flying a helicopter isn't easier than piloting an airplane. The European flight schools that Jennifer looked at required anywhere from 45 to 60 hours of flight time, seven written exams, and a radio test. Even people who already hold airplane pilot licenses must fly an additional 39 hours in a helicopter before they can test for the license.

In 1994, Jennifer received her helicopter pilot's license. She heard that only three men had traveled around the world with a helicopter, and they had used autopilot. Jennifer made the trip in 1997 with a copilot and became the first woman to circumnavigate the globe in a helicopter. At the same time, she raised $100,000 for Save the Children. This first trip was a latitudinal journey from east to west. She did it again in 2000 by herself and without autopilot. She was the first person, male or female, to take a piston-engine helicopter around the world.

Jennifer does more than set records. She also enters races, such as the London to Sydney Air Race of 2001 in which she placed third. She has also run races, such as the 250-kilometer (155 mile) race across the Namib Desert supporting the Scott Polar Research Institute, which she attempted at age 69.

Many of Jennifer's adventures, whether in a helicopter or on foot, benefit charities such as Operation Smile and SOS Children's Villages.

LEARN MORE

Now Solo: One Woman's Record-Breaking Flight Around the World by Jennifer Murray (Mainstream Publishing, 2002)

Polar First website, www.polarfirst.com

Polar First by Jennifer Murray (PPP Company, 2008)

≣ IDA VAN SMITH ≣

Teaching Children to Fly

IMAGINE A GROUP OF CHILDREN, both boys and girls, on an airfield, with lots of bright smiles and perhaps more than a few lips trembling with fear. Chances are, all eyes are big with wonder. They take trips to airports, visit aerospace museums, and learn how to do preflight checks. Many get to ride in a real airplane. Often it's the first airplane ride they have ever taken.

Welcome to an Ida Van Smith Flight Club gathering, where minority children can learn to fly.

Ida Van Smith opened her clubs because she wanted children to have opportunities that took her half a century to experience. She said, "I believe that anything children do very young, they will probably be able to learn better and feel more at ease with than if they wait and they were my age to begin."

Learning to fly airplanes had been her dream since she saw her first one at the age of three. Being both African American and female meant that there was more standing in the way of that dream, but she never forgot it.

Finally, in 1967, 50-year-old grandmother and teacher Ida Van Smith took flying lessons. She had looked into classes at Butler Aviation School at LaGuardia Airport in New York, but she received too many stares. She decided to shop around and found an instructor she liked at Fayetteville's Grannis Field Airport in her home state of North Carolina.

After she earned her pilot's license and instructor rating, this history and special education teacher opened a flight club in Long Island, New York. With a grant from the FAA, she was able to get an aircraft simulator. She provided a Cessna 172. Ida was the first African American female flight instructor in New York and the first African American female pilot from North Carolina.

Once per month during the 1970s, Smith held workshops at York College in Jamaica, New York. She invited air-traffic controllers, commercial pilots, airplane mechanics, and other people in aviation to talk with students from the Ida Van Smith Flight Clubs.

Funding for the program often came from Ida's own pockets in the early days. But word of Ida's schools caught on and spread. More than 20 schools opened in locations in New York, North Carolina, Texas, and St. Lucia in the Caribbean. Thousands of young people from ages 3 to 19 have experienced aviation through the Ida Van Smith Flight Clubs, and many have gone on to aviation careers with airlines or in the military.

Born in Lumberton, North Carolina, in 1917, Ida remembered her father taking her to see a barnstorming exhibition at the airport when she was three or four years old. It was an image that stayed with her. She was fascinated by aviation, but it would be almost 50 years before she became a licensed pilot. She founded the Ida Van Smith Flight Clubs in 1967, introducing children and young adults to the careers that aviation and space had to offer.

Ida moved to New York City after graduating from Shaw University in Raleigh, North Carolina, in the 1940s. She earned her master's degree at Queens College in New York City and began teaching in New York City's schools. Ida also hosted a cable-television show on aviation and taught introductory aviation at York College of the City University of New York. She wrote articles for aviation and education journals in addition to a newspaper column titled, "Come Fly with Me." She was honored many times for her contributions to education and aviation, including becoming the first African American woman inducted into the International Forest of Friendship in Atchison, Kansas.

With her belief that you're never too young to learn about aviation, Ida also created the *Fly with Me Coloring Book*. The 32-page coloring book has a story about flying within its pages.

Retiring from teaching in 1977, Ida remained active with her flight schools and the flying groups she was a member of—Ninety-Nines, Black Wings, and Negro Airmen International—until her death in 2003. The Ida Van Smith Flight Clubs (sometimes known as the Ida Van Smith-Dunn flight clubs) have earned many honors for their work with youth.

Youth Flight Clubs

The Ida Van Smith Flight Clubs aren't the only clubs dedicated to introducing aviation to children. The Royal Air Force of Great Britain sponsors the Air Cadets Organisation for young people between 13 and 20 years of age. Not only are students introduced to aviation, but the Air Cadets program also provides training.

The program actually has a long history, starting in 1859, girls were not allowed to join until the early 1980s. A similar program operates in Canada: the Royal Canadian Air Cadets. Operating in other places throughout the world are the Experimental Aircraft Association Young Eagles programs for 8- to 17-year-olds. The program starts with a free flight and then offers different steps for young people interested in aviation. Smaller programs are offered in various communities. For instance, the Bronze Eagles Flying Club was started about 45 years ago by African American pilots in Houston but has spread throughout Texas and Arkansas. The club's goal is to expose African American youth to the possibilities of aviation through an annual fly-in event and a two-week Summer Flight Academy. The Summer Flight Academy teaches 16 high school students how to fly. Some of the participants, such as Decarla Greaves, have gone on to careers in aviation.

LEARN MORE

American Women and Flight Since 1940 by Deborah G. Douglas, Amy E. Foster, Alan D. Meyer, and Lucy B. Young (University Press of Kentucky, 2004)

"Ida Van Smith" on the Smithsonian National Air and Space Museum website, http://airandspace.si.edu/explore-and -learn/topics/women/SmithV.cfm

⧏ JERRIE COBB ⧐
Missionary Pilot

JERRIE COBB MAY HAVE started piloting airplanes younger than any other woman. She flew her father's 1936 Waco bi-wing when she was 12 years old. She loved flying the plane with her father, Lieutenant Colonel William H. Cobb, by her side.

———•———

Born in Norman, Oklahoma, on March 5, 1931, Geraldyn "Jerrie" Cobb was the younger of two daughters. Within weeks of her birth, the family moved to Washington, DC, where her grandfather was a congressman. Due to World War II and her father's service in the National Guard, the family also moved to other places during her childhood.

As a child, she enjoyed sleeping in the backyard and looking at the stars. She had traded her blond pigtails for a blond
ponytail by the time she earned her private pilot's license at age
16, which was the earliest age at which a person could get one.
Still attending an Oklahoma City high school, she spent her
spare time at the airfield, performing odd jobs such as wash-
ing and waxing planes in exchange for flying time. During her
16th summer, she barnstormed across the Midwest in a Piper
Cub. Her first job after high school was flying a Piper Cub over
towns, dropping circulars.

Jerrie spent one year in college before quitting. She already
knew what she wanted to do: fly. She played semiprofessional
softball for the Oklahoma City Queens to raise enough money
to buy a Fairchild PT-23, a World War II surplus plane. With a
commercial license at age 18, Jerrie began crop dusting, flying
charters, and patrolling oil pipelines while she worked on her
flight instructor's license. By 21, she was giving flight instruction.

Always ready for an adventure, Jerrie took a job ferrying
military planes and bombers for the Peruvian Air Force in 1953.
She got the job because male pilots thought it was too risky. She
crossed shark-infested waters, Andean mountains, and jungles.
Once, while refueling in Ecuador, she was arrested on suspicion
of being a spy.

Back in Oklahoma at age 24, she began setting world altitude,
speed, and distance records. She set an altitude record of 30,300
feet (9,240 meters) and a world distance record from Guatemala
City to Oklahoma City in a twin-engine Aero Commander. The
records had previously been held by Soviet military pilots. In all,
Jerrie earned four world aviation records for light planes.

Like Jackie Cochran, Jerrie broke the sound barrier; her
experience was with a TR-102 Delta Dagger. She learned to fly
the Bell helicopter after 83 minutes of instruction and became

the first female test pilot for Aero Design and Engineering Company.

By the time she was 28, she had logged about 10,000 flight hours. The National Pilot's Association also presented her with the Harmon Trophy as the world's best female pilot. The same year, she was named "Woman of the Year" by the Women's National Aeronautic Association. Along with the Amelia Earhart Gold Medal of Achievement, Jerrie received dozens of awards during her flying career.

When NASA started investigating the possibility of female astronauts in the late 1950s and early 1960s, Jerrie Cobb was its first choice. Not only did she have twice as many flight hours as astronaut John Glenn, she had piloted 64 types of aircraft. She passed all 75 tests, scoring in the top 2 percent of all male or female astronaut candidates. When the government shut the program down, Jerrie spoke before Congress and tried to convince them to change their minds—without success. They asked her to be a NASA consultant, but after two years of receiving no consulting work, she quit.

Disappointed, 32-year-old Jerrie took her aviation skills to new and unknown territory—the Amazon rainforest, an area that is larger than the United States. The natives called her plane, a twin-engine Britten-Norman Islander, "the bird." Her landing strip was small, surrounded by 200-foot (61 meter) trees. The jungle is a difficult place to fly. Even taking off is a challenge, as a pilot must pull up quickly without stalling the engine.

The Amazon rainforest was one of the last wild places on Earth to which Jerrie could go. She carried with her antibiotics and other medicines, doctors, clothing, and seeds to grow into food for millions of people. When needed, she located downed aircraft. One day, Jerrie sat with the young chief of a village who was dying of meningitis, a white man's disease that was unknown to the native population. She felt helpless as he lay dying. She began a foundation to buy medicine and crop seeds for the people she served. She took on special projects as well. At one time, she returned displaced Miskito people back to their homes in Nicaragua.

Jerrie made humanitarian trips to Amazonia, as South America's rainforest area is sometimes known, for 35 years. She was honored by the governments of Brazil, Peru, and Colombia for humanitarian flying to serve the indigenous people. Colombia even gave her an honorary rank in the Colombian Air Force. The government of Ecuador honored Jerrie in 1965 for pioneering new air routes through the Amazon. Twenty years later, Central and South American groups were still singing her praises for her lifesaving jungle flights.

For almost thirty-five years, she lived in remote villages in Central and South America. Her primary area was the land where Colombia, Brazil, and Venezuela meet; the people there spend most of their daytime hours searching for food, primarily cassava, a starchy root. At night she would sleep in a hammock in a *maloca*, a communal home covered with palm leaves that houses 60 to 80 Indians. Canoes were the primary mode of transportation other than walking. Jerrie used her phenomenal aviation skills to improve the lives of millions of people and was nominated for a Nobel Peace Prize for her work in 1981.

In 1998, former astronaut John Glenn returned to space on a mission that would study the effects of space travel on older adults. NASA didn't realize what it was taking on by planning this new mission. Several members of the Mercury 13, the group of women who were to undergo astronaut training in the early 1960s, protested. They had waited more than 40 years for their first opportunity to go into space, and John Glenn was going a second time.

The story of the Mercury 13 received attention, and women such as Jerrie Cobb won a new group of admirers who agreed it was Jerrie's turn to go to space. It was enough to bring her home from the Amazon. She called going into space her destiny. "I've thought about it all my life. I will do whatever it takes."

A campaign began. People began contacting NASA and Congress, sending them T-shirts that said, WOMEN FLY. They circulated petitions, collecting more than 15,000 signatures. The First Lady at the time, Hillary Clinton, asked Daniel Goldin of NASA to meet with Jerrie. Goldin was in charge of astronaut selection and had received the petitions. Jerrie dared to get her hopes up one more time, but Goldin said they had enough astronauts.

Today, Jerrie has flown more than 55,000 hours and continues to fly. She is in excellent physical condition from her time in the Amazon. If she could have one thing, it would be the opportunity that was denied to her more than 50 years ago. She wants to fly the ultimate flight—into space. Until then, she's content to remain in the Amazon jungles and help others. In doing so, she said, she feels like the luckiest woman in the world.

LEARN MORE

Jerrie Cobb Foundation website, www.jerrie-cobb.org

Jerrie Cobb, Solo Pilot by Jerrie Cobb (Jerrie Cobb Foundation, 1997)

⧦ ACKNOWLEDGMENTS ⧦

MANY YEARS AGO, I BECAME acquainted with Bessie Coleman in a museum exhibit. I had never heard of this fascinating woman, who had done so much in such a short time, and that's unfortunate. Bessie Coleman is a name we should all know, as is Jerrie Cobb and the names of all the other amazing women featured in this book. Telling their stories in this book was an honor and a privilege for me. I'm only sorry that I couldn't feature even more women aviators.

I am deeply indebted to the Ninety-Nines, Inc. International Organization of Women Pilots. In the years that I've been learning and writing about women aviators, their artifacts and resources have been invaluable. (If you're ever in the Oklahoma City area, you should stop by the Ninety-Nines Museum of Women Pilots near the airport.) Special thanks goes to Laura Ohrenberg from the Ninety-Nines headquarters.

Another incredible resource has been Texas Woman's University. Its Woman's Collection included a vast amount of information about women in aviation, Women Airforce Service Pilots, and the Whirly-Girls organization.

And finally, thank you to Jerome Pohlen and all the great people at Chicago Review Press for allowing me the opportunity to write about what fascinates me.

≣ NOTES ≣

Introduction

The reference to Katharine Wright as "the third Wright brother" is located at the Wright Brothers Aeroplane Company at www .wright-brothers.org/Information_Desk/Just_the_Facts /Wright_Family/Katharine_Wright/Katharine_Wright.htm.

The quote attributed to Clare Boothe Luce comes from the Clare Boothe Luce biography at the Henry Luce Foundation website, www.hluce.org/cblbio.aspx.

Part I: Pioneers of Aviation

Baroness de Laroche

Elise de Laroche's quote about her flight for Tsar Nicholas II came from an article she wrote, published in *Collier's Magazine*, volume 48, September 20, 1911. The article's title was "Flying in Presence of the Czar."

Harriet Quimby

Harriet's description of her history-making flight came from an article she wrote for *Leslie's Illustrated Weekly*. "An American Girl's Daring Exploit" appeared in the magazine on May 16, 1912.

Her article, "How a Woman Learns to Fly," also appeared in *Leslie's*. It was published May 25, 1911.

Part II: The Golden Age of Flight

Louise Thaden's quote about the Women's Air Derby comes from her autobiography, *High, Wide, and Frightened* (page 51).

The quote about the first Ninety-Nines meeting comes from a November 2, 1929, article in the *New York Times*.

Amelia Earhart

Amelia Earhart's last words are featured in many locations, including her official website, www.ameliaearhart.com/about/bio2.html.

Earhart's statement to Louise Thaden is featured on the Amelia Earhart Birthplace Museum website, www.ameliaearhart museum.org/AmeliaEarhart/AEAviator.htm.

Louise Thaden

Louise Thaden's quotes about winning the Bendix come from her autobiography, *High, Wide, and Frightened*.

Elinor Smith

The Elinor Smith quotes come from her autobiography, *Aviatrix*.

Edna Gardner Whyte

The quotes by Edna Gardner Whyte come from her autobiography, *Rising Above It: An Autobiography*.

Beryl Markham

The quote about the Atlantic Crossing came from an account of her trip that she wrote for the *Daily Express*. It was repeated on http://library.thinkquest.org/21229/bio/bmark.htm.

Willa Brown

Details of Willa Brown's trip to the *Chicago Defender* come from a Smithsonian National Air and Space Museum Teacher Guide, "African American Pioneers in Aviation, 1920–Present," page 14.

Part III: Wartime and Military Flying

Vi Cowden's quote about the disbanding of the WASPs comes from her interview with the Veterans History Project of the American Folklife Center.

Jacqueline Cochran

Jacqueline Cochran's quote comes from the book *Flying for Her Country: The American & Soviet Women Military Pilots of World War I* by Amy Goodpaster Strebe (Westport, CT: Praeger Security International, 2007).

Violet Cowden

Quotes come from Violet Cowden's interview with the Veterans History Project of the American Folklife Center from the Library of Congress and the documentary *Fly Girls*.

Valentina Grizodubova

Valentina Grizodubova's quote comes from the book *Flying for Her Country: The American & Soviet Women Military Pilots of World War II* by Amy Goodpaster Strebe (Westport, CT: Praeger Security International, 2007).

Hanna Reitsch

Quotes from Hanna Reitsch come from *Nazi Test Pilot to Hitler's Bunker* by Dennis Piszkiewicz (Westport, CT: Praeger, 1997).

Part IV: All Part of the Job

Pancho Barnes

The information about attending a flight exhibition with her grandfather come from the Pancho Barnes Official Website, www.panchobarnes.com.

Pancho's quote "Choose Happy" was mentioned on the Pancho Barnes Official Website, www.panchobarnes.com.

The information about the interview with the reporter around the time of the Powder Puff Derby came from *Powder Puff Derby: Petticoat Pilots and Flying Flappers* by Mike Walker, (West Sussex, England: Wiley Press, 2003).

Patty Wagstaff

Quotes come from the article "Patty Wagstaff's Second Act" by Debbie Gary, published in *Air and Space* magazine, August 2011.

Part V: Making a Difference

Details about Patricia Mawuli came from the *World* newspaper, "Patricia Mawuli: Ghana's High-Flying Woman," June 11, 2012, www.theworld.org/2012/06/patricia-mawuli-ghanas -high-flying-woman.

Ruth Nichols

The quote from Ruth Nichols comes from the National Aviation Hall of Fame website, www.nationalaviation.org/nichols-ruth.

Jennifer Murray

Quotes come from the talk she gave for TEDx, which is called "Jennifer Murray—Survival Against the Odds" and can be found at TEDxTalks, http://tedxtalks.ted.com/video/TEDxH KUST-Jennifer-Murray-Survi;search%3AJennifer%20Murray. TED is a nonprofit organization that sponsors programs that fit the tagline "Ideas Worth Spreading" from three areas: technology, entertainment, and design.

Ida Van Smith

Ida Van Smith's quote about children learning aviation comes from an interview with the *Robesonian*, printed on May 11, 2003. The article by Jim Rathgeber is titled "Liftoff: 'Dreams of Flight' Exhibit Opens Wednesday at Robeson Museum," and the quote is on page 7C.

Jerrie Cobb

The quote about the space program is from an interview with the *Oklahoman* newspaper, "State-Born Aviatrix Yearns for Space" by Ann DeFrange.

☰ GLOSSARY ☰

aerialist: A person who performs in the air, such as on a trapeze or on an airplane. Barnstormers sometimes had people walking on wings and trying other moves outside of planes while they were in the air.

aerobatics: Expert and sometimes dangerous movements performed by aircraft in the sky.

aeronautics: The science of aircraft of all kinds, from airplanes to rockets, including design, construction, and repair.

altitude: The height of something from the ground. Altitude records were popular in the early days of aviation.

Army Air Forces: This US military branch was in charge of military flying during World War II. More than 2.4 million people served in the Army Air Forces. It later became the US Air Force.

barnstorming: Performing exhibition or stunt flying, often in small towns or rural areas.

biplane: An airplane that has two sets of wings instead of one set, as found in monoplanes.

bush pilot: A bush pilot serves in remote areas of Africa, Australia, or the Arctic tundra. Due to the hostile flying environment, a bush pilot must be very skilled. Planes most suited for this kind of flying usually have high wings and taildragger landing gear. Taildraggers, also known as conventional landing gear, have two large forward wheels and one wheel at the back of the plane. Because of the short runways common in remote areas, bush planes usually have high-lift devices. Some bush planes have floats or skis that allow them to operate on water or snow.

Caudron: The Caudron Airplane Company was an early and famous French aircraft company founded by brothers, Gaston and René Caudron. The Caudron brothers also operated a flight school in France. The aircraft company also produced planes for World War I and World War II.

Cessna: An aircraft manufacturing company based in Wichita, Kansas, and founded by Clyde Cessna, who built his first airplane in 1911. In 1924, he partnered with Walter Beech and Lloyd C. Stearman to create Travel Air, a manufacturer of biplanes. A few years later, Cessna left and started his own company, Cessna Aircraft Company, focusing on monoplanes. Cessna Aircraft Company became a leading producer of light aircraft. It now produces single-engine airplanes and business jets.

Civil Aeronautics Authority (CAA): A regulatory agency governing civil aviation. In the United States, many of the CAA's duties were transferred to the Federal Aviation Administration. Other countries also have agencies to regulate aviation.

Civil Air Patrol (CAP): A voluntary aviation agency that began in the late 1930s to assist with defense efforts in the United States. The CAP later became part of the US Air Force

Auxiliary. It continues today by providing emergency services, education, and cadet programs.

cub: A Piper Cub airplane. This light aircraft was produced from the 1930s to the 1980s.

derby: Although a derby is a type of hat, it is also a race. Horse races are often called derbies—for example, the Kentucky Derby. Some air races also used the term "derby," such as the Women's Air Derby.

endurance: The ability to last at something for a long time. Endurance records joined speed and altitude records as important in aviation during the first half of the 20th century.

exhibition: A public display of something. In early aviation, people gathered to watch airplanes take off and fly in exhibitions.

fascism: A form of government in which the leader, known as a dictator, has complete control of the country. During World War II, both Italy and Germany were ruled by fascism.

Federal Aviation Administration (FAA): A government organization within the Department of Transportation that sets and oversees standards for aircraft, regulates air traffic, inspects aircraft, and investigates accidents.

flyer: Early airplanes, specifically the first powered aircraft by the Wright brothers, were called flyers.

glider: A light aircraft that flies by using air currents instead of engines. Gliders became popular in Germany after World War I, as Germany was not allowed to build military-type aircraft.

knickerbockers: Loose-fitting trousers that fit at the knee.

license: A document that gives a person permission to do something. A pilot's license gives the owner permission to fly an airplane. Some specific aviation licenses include student, private, sport, and commercial licenses.

Lockheed: An American aerospace company originally founded in 1912 as Loughead Aircraft Manufacturing Company. In 1926, it became Lockheed Aircraft Company and later Lockheed Corporation. Its first successful aircraft was the Vega, used by aviators such as Amelia Earhart and Wiley Post. Their Electra model was used in Earhart's around-the-world flight and later as a base for various military aircraft for the United States and Great Britain. In all, Lockheed produced 6 percent of the military aircraft in World War II. After the war, Lockheed began developing airliners for companies such as Trans-World Airlines (TWA), but it also continued a military division for which it developed jet fighters and military transports. In 1995, Lockheed merged with Martin Marietta and became known as Lockheed Martin.

Mach: A unit for measuring the speed of aircraft, named after Austrian physicist Ernst Mach. Mach actually shows flight velocity and depends on the altitudes. Mach 1 at sea level is 761 miles per hour (1,224 kilometers per hour). This is also known as the speed of sound. Mach 2 is twice the speed of sound.

monoplane: An airplane with one set of wings.

pilot-in-command: The person in charge of the aircraft while flying. This is often the captain of the plane in airliners and military aircraft.

pursuit plane: A pursuit plane is a military fighter airplane created for air-to-air combat.

ratings: Certifications among pilots that determine what types of airplanes they are able to fly. Ratings can be based on the type of plane, such as glider or helicopter. Ratings can also refer to instrument rating, which is an advanced rating that demonstrates that a pilot is capable of flying in unfamiliar locations or in adverse conditions.

sound barrier: This is related to the speed of sound, or Mach 1. If an aircraft is passing through the sound barrier, it moves faster than sound does. When airplanes first began "breaking" the sound barrier, it created a shock wave that made a booming sound. This doesn't happen as often, as there are rules about how fast pilots can fly.

taxi: For airplanes, "taxi" means to move along the ground before takeoff or after landing.

transport pilot: A certification that is the highest rating a pilot can hold. For US pilots, this means also being a commercial pilot with an instrument rating.

tsar: A Russian emperor; this leader was a member of Russia's royalty, who led the country. The word is also sometimes spelled "czar." The Russian Revolution of 1917 ended the system of tsars.

WAFS: The Women's Auxiliary Ferrying Squadron was created in 1942 to ferry trainers and light aircraft from factories. Initially supervised by Nancy Harkness Love, it was later incorporated into the Women's Airforce Service Pilots (WASP).

WAVES: Women Accepted for Volunteer Emergency Service. An auxiliary organization operated by the navy to release male navy personnel for duty during World War II. With a group of 86,000 women, the WAVES assisted with air-traffic control, air navigation, communication, and clerical work. The WAVES operated between 1942 and 1948.

≡ BIBLIOGRAPHY ≡

Books for Adults

Bell, Elizabeth S. *Sisters of the Wind: Voices of Early Women Aviators.* Pasadena, CA: Trilogy Books, 1994.

Carl, Ann B. *A WASP Among Eagles: A Woman Military Test Pilot in World War II.* Washington, DC: Smithsonian Institution Press, 2010.

Cochran, Jacqueline, and Mary Ann Bucknum Brinley. *Jackie Cochran: Autobiography.* New York: Bantam Books, 1987.

Freydberg, Elizabeth Hadley. *Bessie Coleman: The Brownskin Lady Bird.* New York: Garland Publishing, 1994.

Hall, Ed Y. *Harriet Quimby: America's First Lady of the Air.* Spartanburg, SC: Honoribus Press, 1997.

Hoppes, Jonna Doolittle. *Just Doing My Job: Stories of Service from World War II.* Santa Monica, CA: Santa Monica Press, 2009.

Jaros, Dean. *Heroes Without Legacy: American Airwomen, 1912–1944.* Niwot, CO: University Press of Colorado, 1994.

Kessler, Lauren. *The Happy Bottom Riding Club: The Life and Times of Pancho Barnes.* New York: Random House, 2000.

Marck, Bernard. *Women Aviators: From Amelia Earhart to Sally Ride, Making History in Air and Space.* New York: Flammarion, 2009.

Markham, Beryl. *West with the Night.* Reprint, San Francisco: North Point Press, 1983.

Piszkiewicz, Dennis. *Nazi Test Pilot to Hitler's Bunker.* Westport, CT: Praeger, 1997.

Rich, Doris L. *Queen Bess: Daredevil Aviator.* Washington, DC: Smithsonian Institution Press, 1995.

Russo, Carolyn. *Women and Flight: Portraits of Contemporary Women Pilots.* Boston: National Air and Space Museum Smithsonian Institution and Bulfinch Press/Little, Brown, 1997.

Scott, Phil. *The Pioneers of Flight: A Documentary History.* Princeton, NJ: Princeton University Press, 1999.

Smith, Elinor. *Aviatrix.* New York: Thorndike Press, 1982.

Snook Southern, Neta. *I Taught Amelia to Fly.* New York: Vantage Press, 1974.

Strebe, Amy Goodpaster. *Flying for Her Country: The American and Soviet Women Military Pilots of World War II.* Westport, CT: Praeger Security International, 2007.

Thaden, Louise McPhetridge. *High, Wide, and Frightened.* Reprint, Fayetteville, AR: University of Arkansas Press, 2005.

Veca, Donna. *Just Plane Crazy: Biography of Bobbi Trout.* Santa Clara, CA: Osborne Publisher, 1987.

Walker, Mike. *Powder Puff Derby: Petticoat Pilots and Flying Flappers.* West Sussex, England: Wiley Press, 2004.

Wels, Susan. *Amelia Earhart: The Thrill of It.* Philadelphia: Running Press, 2009.

Whyte, Edna Gardner and Ann L. Cooper. *Rising Above It: An Autobiography.* New York: Orion Books, 1991.

Books for Children

Brown, Tami Lewis, and François Roca. *Soar, Elinor!* New York: Farrar, Straus and Giroux, 2010.

McLoone, Margo. *Women Explorers of the Air: Harriet Quimby, Bessie Coleman, Amelia Earhart, Beryl Markham, Jacqueline Cochran.* Minneapolis: Capstone Press, 1999.

Rimmerman, Sara. *Hidden Heroine—Fay Gillis Wells.* Reston, VA: Zeus Enterprises, 1999.

Newspapers and Magazines

Aviation for Women (magazine)

Burstein, Jennifer. "She Reached for the Sky to Become America's First Chinese-American Female Pilot." *Audrey Magazine,* December 2005.

Church, Ellen. "Flying Brings Life of Enrichment." *Robesonian,* January 23, 1995.

Crow, Kelly. "Breaking Barriers." *Oklahoma Today* 48, no. 5 (July–August 1998).

"Female Aviation Pioneer to Share Her Fervor for Flight at Stephens College." *Missourian,* March 20, 2012.

Flying for Freedom: The Story of the Women Airforce Service Pilots (Teacher Resource Guide). NMUSAF Education Division.

Grosscup, Luann. "Fly Girls: WASPS Carried the Non-Combat Load When the Boys Were 'Over There.'" *Chicago Tribune,* May 23, 1999.

Jameson, Tonya. "Pilots Meet to Mark Opening of First Exhibition of Women Pilots." *Boca Raton News,* June 13, 1997.

Lambertson, Giles. "The Other Harlem." *Air and Space Magazine,* March 2010.

Lee, Renée C. "Flying Club Inspires Youth to Soar." *Houston Chronicle,* February 7, 2012.

Manning, Elizabeth. "Duo Celebrate 40th Anniversary of Woman's Polar Flight." *Anchorage Daily News,* August 4, 2003.

Mortimer, Gavin. "Beryl Markham: Britain's Amelia Earhart." *Telegraph,* November 27, 2009.

Moses, Phyllis R. "The Amazing Aviatrix Elinor Smith." *Woman Pilot,* March 30, 2008.

Oakes, Claudia M. "United States Women in Aviation 1930–1939." *Smithsonian Studies in Air and Space,* no. 6 (1985).

Robinson, Danielle. "Flying Gran's Record High." *Manchester Evening News,* June 8, 2007.

Tillman, Judith. "Flying: Lifelong Interest for Aviatrix-Grandmother." *Robesonian,* January 2, 1979.

"Wally Funk Suited for Space." *State Magazine* 5, no. 1 (Fall 2009).

Woo, Elaine. "Katherine Cheung, 98; Immigrant Was Nation's First Licensed Asian American Woman Pilot." *Los Angeles Times*, September 7, 2003.

Videos and DVDs

Bessie Coleman. Texan Cultures. YouTube.
Bessie Coleman: The Fly Girls. Epworth Foundation. YouTube.
Black Wings: The First Female African American Pilot. Smithsonian Channel. YouTube.
Breaking Through the Clouds: The First Women's National Air Derby (Film). Archetypal Images. Heather Taylor, Director. 2010.
Captain Beverly Burns Receives Amelia Earhart Award. Rob and Beverly Burns. YouTube.
Champion Aerobatic Pilot Patty Wagstaff. Moving Art. YouTube.
"Elinor Smith Breaks Woman's Altitude Record at Roosevelt Field in New York." Critical Past. www.criticalpast.com/video /65675041967_Elinor-Smith_aircraft-takes-off_altitude-record _airplane_Roosevelt-Field.
Fly Girls. American Experience, PBS. Laurel Ladevich, Director. WGBH Educational Foundation, 1999.
Jennifer Murray: Survival Against the Odds. TedX. YouTube.
Notes of Hope: Lynn Ripplemeyer. Medical Bridges. YouTube.
Wings of Silver: The Vi Cowden Story (documentary). Mark C. Bonn, Christine Seiber Bonn, Directors, 2010.
"Wright Brothers Demonstrate Flight with a Passenger in Le Mans, France." Critical Past. www.criticalpast.com/video/65675026656 _Wright-brothers_drawn-by-horses_pull-weight-of-launching -derrick_sits-with-a-passenger.

Websites

Air Ambulance Service, "The History of the Air Ambulance": www .airambulanceservice.com/history.html
AOPA, Aircraft Owners and Pilots Association: www.aopa.org

Air Race Classic: www.airraceclassic.org/historyt.asp

Amelia Earhart Birthplace Museum: www.ameliaearhartmuseum
.org

Amelia Earhart Official Website: http://ameliaearhart.com

Ames Historical Society, "Neta Snook": www.ameshistoricalsociety
.org/exhibits/snook.htm

Angel Flight: www.angelflight.com

Aviation Museum of Kentucky, "Willa Brown Chappell": www.ket
.org/trips/aviation/chappell.htm

AvStop Online Magazine, "Russian Women Pilots": http://avstop
.com/history/aroundtheworld/russia/nexen.htm

Bessie Coleman: www.bessiecoleman.com

Bobbi Trout—Aviatrix: The Official Web Site of the American Leg-
end: www.bobbitrout.com

A Bridge of Wings: http://bridgeofwings.com/

A Brief Flight, "Hazel Ying Lee": www.hazelyinglee.com/main.html

British Air Transport Auxiliary: www.airtransportaux.com/index
.html

California State Military Museum, "Florence L. 'Pancho' Barnes":
www.militarymuseum.org/Barnes.html

Century of Flight: www.century-of-flight.net

China History Forum, "History of Aviation in a China That Never Was":
www.chinahistoryforum.com/index.php?/topic/29274-history
-of-aviation-in-a-china-that-never-was

City Noise, "The Bridges of New York City": http://citynoise.org
/article/773

Civil Air Patrol: www.gocivilairpatrol.com

CNN, "Equal Opportunities at 38,000 Feet": www.cnn.com/2010
/WORLD/asiapcf/10/28/malaysia.female.pilots/index.html

———, "Why Aren't More Women Airline Pilots?": http://articles
.cnn.com/2011-03-18/travel/female.airline.pilots_1_women
-airline-pilots-american-airlines-captain-helen-richey
?_s=PM:TRAVEL

Cradle of Aviation Museum, "People": www.cradleofaviation.org
/history/people

Davis-Monthan Aviation Field Register, "Florence Low 'Pancho' Barnes": http://dmairfield.org/people/barnes_fl/
————, "Lady Mary Heath": www.dmairfield.com/people/heath_lm
Dwight D. Eisenhower Presidential Library and Museum, "Jacqueline Cochran and the Women's Airforce Service Pilots (WASPs): http://eisenhower.archives.gov/research/online_documents /jacqueline_cochran.html
EAA, "EAA's Countdown to Kitty Hawk": www.countdowntokitty hawk.com
EAA Young Eagles: www.youngeagles.org
Eagle Flight Squadron, Inc.: http://eagleflightsquadron.org
Early Aviators, "Baroness de Laroche": http://earlyaviators.com /edelaroc.htm
Edwards Air Force Base, "Team Edwards Celebrates Pancho Barnes Day": www.edwards.af.mil/news/story.asp?id=123177234
Encyclopedia of Arkansas History and Culture, "Louise McPhetridge Thaden (1905–1979)": http://encyclopediaofarkansas.net /encyclopedia/entry-detail.aspx?entryID=30
Federal Aviation Administration (FAA): http://earlyaviators.com /edelaroc.htm
FAI, "The First Women's Records": www.fai.org/records/57-fai/35098 -the-first-womens-records
First Flight Foundation, "Honoring 100 Aviation Heroes": www .firstflightfoundation.org/first-flight-foundation-about-us/first -flight-foundation-history/honoring-100-aviation-heroes.shtml
Gale Group, "Beryl Markham": www.karenblixen.com/gale.html
Goldstripes Aviation, "Centennial of Women Pilots": http://centennial ofwomenpilots.com
Hill Air Force Base, "Willa Brown": www.hill.af.mil/library/fact sheets/factsheet.asp?id=5858
International Forest of Friendship: http://ifof.org
International Society of Women Airline Pilots: www.iswap.org
International Women's Air and Space Museum: http://iwasm.org /wp-blog

Iowa Pathways, "Neta Snook: Determined to Fly": www.iptv.org
/iowapathways/mypath.cfm?ounid=ob_000185

Jerrie Cobb Foundation: www.jerrie-cobb.org

Library of Congress, American Folklife Center Veterans History
Project, "Interview with Violet Cowden": http://lcweb2.loc.gov
/diglib/vhp/story/loc.natlib.afc2001001.18240/transcript?ID
=sr0001

Lindbergh Foundation, "Lindbergh Foundation Partners with
the Patty Wagstaff Kenya Wildlife Service": www.lindbergh
foundation.org/docs/index.php/patty-wagstaff

Motion Picture Pilots Association, "Patty Wagstaff": www.movie
pilots.com/members/wagstaff.html

National Aviation Hall of Fame, "Enshrinees": www.nationalaviation
.org/enshrinees

National Museum of the US Air Force (Fact Sheets): www.national
museum.af.mil

National WASP World War II Museum, "Jackie Cochran Biography":
http://waspmuseum.org/jackie-cochran-biography/NASA

———, "Elinor Smith: Born to Fly": www.nasa.gov/topics/people
/features/elinor-smith.html

———, "Gliders": www.grc.nasa.gov/WWW/k-12/airplane/glider
.html

The Ninety-Nines Inc. International Organization of Women Pilots:
www.ninety-nines.org

Oklahoma Historical Society's Encyclopedia of Oklahoma History
and Culture, "Geraldyn M. Cobb": http://digital.library.okstate
.edu/encyclopedia/entries/C/CO010.html

Pancho Barnes Official Website: www.panchobarnes.com

Patty Wagstaff Airshows: www.pattywagstaff.com

Polar First: www.polarfirst.com

Royal Air Force Air Cadets: www.raf.mod.uk/aircadets

San Diego Air and Space Museum: www.sandiegoairandspace.org

Smithsonian Air and Space Museum, "America by Air": http://airand
space.si.edu/exhibitions/gal102/americabyair/index.cfm

———, "Black Wings": http://airandspace.si.edu/blackwings

———, "Women in Aviation": http://airandspace.si.edu/explore-and
-learn/topics/women/roche.cfm

Society of Air Racing Historians, "Results of the Bendix Air Race":
www.airrace.com/ResultsBendix.htm

South Central Section Ninety-Nines, "Wally Funk Is Still Determined to Get Her Shot at Space": www.scs99s.org/Profiles
/WallyFunk.pdf

Texas Woman's University Libraries and Digital Collections: www
.twu.edu/library/wasp.asp

TIGHAR (The International Group for Historical Aircraft Recovery):
http://tighar.org

University of North Carolina–Greensboro, Betty H. Carter Women
Veterans Historical Project, "Violet Cowden Papers": http://
library.uncg.edu/dp/wv/collection.aspx?col=450

University of Wisconsin–Oshkosh, "Mercury 13": www.uwosh.edu
/mercury13

US Air Force (Fact Sheets; News): www.af.mil

Whirly-Girls: www.whirlygirls.org

Wings Across America: http://wingsacrossamerica.us/

"Women in Aviation and Space History": http://airandspace.si.edu
/explore-and-learn/topics/women/

Wright Brothers Aeroplane Company: www.wright-brothers.org

≣ INDEX ≣